Music: The Therapeutic Edge

Readings
from
William W. Sears

Edited by
Margaret S. Sears

Barcelona
PUBLISHERS

Music—The Therapeutic Edge:
Readings from William W. Sears

Copyright © 2007 by Barcelona Publishers

ISBN-10: 1-891278-48-7

ISBN-13: 978-1-891278-48-8

2 4 6 8 9 7 5 3 1

Distributed throughout the world by:
Barcelona Publishers
4 White Brook Road
Gilsum NH 03448
Tel: 603-357-0236 Fax: 603-357-2073
Website: www.barcelonapublishers.com
SAN 298-6299

Cover design:
© 2007 Frank McShane

Acknowledgments

Perhaps the most difficult charge when writing a book is the Acknowledgments section. Where to begin; the fear of forgetting significant helpers; the danger of sounding superficial about something for which one has strong feelings. Larry Dossey approached this fearful problem with much greater eloquence than I in his Acknowledgments to *Reinventing Medicine* when he stated, "Who . . . should I thank for encouragement and support? The list could be infinite, like the mind itself. Perhaps thanks to a few people will spread to all others via the One Mind of which we all are a part" (Dossey, 1999, p. xiii). Echoing Dossey's words, I hope the thanks I extend to those below will spread far and wide via the One Mind to the others who helped bring this endeavor to life.

As the Reverend Homer (Butch) Henderson and I planned Bill's funeral service, Butch said that a copy of something Bill had written would help him "know the man." I sadly shook my head because there was little in print to guide him. Suddenly, I remembered that a partial transcription had been made of a speech presented three years earlier at the 1977 National Association for Music Therapy conference in Anaheim, CA. I gave Butch a copy, and from that simple act arose this work before you. Thus, with sincere gratitude, I thank Butch for setting me on this path.

From the outset, this path was strewn with obstacles. Locating tape recordings of Bill's presentations—no "hard" copies existed—was a Herculean task made easier by the generosity of several people, specifically Gene Morlan, then director of Professional Programs, and Bruce Wilson, Archivist, both at Music Educators National Conference, and Charles T. Eagle. Numerous NAMT friends (some, I fear, who have fallen victim to my faulty memory over time) generously responded to my request for help, although none owned any of the elusive tapes. While my search produced little, I was elated to learn that at least one event, the 1979 second international music therapy symposium held in Dallas, TX, had been transcribed by Sally Hough Smith, the symposium coordinator. It was the only product that came to me in written form, thereby freeing me from the punishing transcribing chore. What a blessing and helpful friend was Sally.

A project of this complexity required a skilled and knowledgeable hand to guide it through turbulent seas, and I was fortunate to have such a friend and colleague as Charles T. Eagle who answered my call. Charles carefully read, critiqued, and edited the complete manuscript—some sections several times—providing sound counsel, insight, and clarification of some of Bill's cryptic remarks which puzzled me. No one could more effectively get inside Bill's mind (a necessary feat) to accurately interpret a number of his statements. Quite simply, this book could not have come to fruition without Charles' masterful assistance. Never will my indebtedness to him be exhausted.

Many times along the way I stumbled, and fancied that the trail was forever lost. It was Roberta [Metzler] Kagin who cleared away the debris and led me to Ken Bruscia and Barcelona Publishers. Ken's patience and encouragement through numerous proofings and several content disappointments buoyed my spirits and kept me moving. It is beyond my "poor power" to find the proper verbal accolades to express my appreciation for the risk he took and the faith he had in Bill's 25-plus year old message and my ability to help tell it.

Elaine Abbott typed and unflinchingly retyped the manuscript until we both got it right, and never complained about my dinosaur computer. I continue to marvel that she was able to order her computer to accurately create Ervin Laszlo's complex model, Emergent Geopolitical Systems (Figure 8, Models for Thinking, Chap. 3). And there were other images that she expertly designed, and skills she demonstrated. Amazing! What a rock she was!

John Buckner, then a member of the Washburn University music faculty in Topeka, worked a miracle or two by locating an old issue of *Music Educators Journal* in the university library when librarians elsewhere had given up. Not to be forgotten are the many librarians at the University of Kansas Library and the Santa Fe Public Library who patiently and expeditiously filled my numerous interlibrary loan requests. No one even flinched or made questionable remarks when I requested the same book twice—or more.

Models play a significant role in this text, and I am grateful for permission from publishers to use several copyrighted images. These are:

Pearson Education, Glenview, IL, for Herbert J. Klausmeier and Willian Goodwin's adaptation of Robert M. Gagne's "Types of Human Learning" model (Figure 1, "Models for Thinking," Chapter 3); their (Klausmeier & Goodwin) schematic arrangement of "Cognitive Abilities and Learning Outcomes" based on J. P. Guilford's "Structure-of-Intellect" theory (Figure 3, "Models for Thinking," Chapter 3); and Morris L. Bigge's model, "Man's Actional Nature" (Figure 4, "Models for Thinking," Chapter 3).

McGraw-Hill Book Co., New York, for J. P. Guilford's "Structure-of-Intellect" model (Figure 2, "Models for Thinking," Chapter 3).

George Braziller, New York, for the intriguing Emergent Geopolitical Systems design by Ervin Laszlo (Figure 8, "Models for Thinking," Chapter 3).

And finally, I wish to thank Prentice Hall, Saddle River, NJ, for permission to reprint "Processes in Music Therapy," Chapter 2 of E. Thayer

Gaston's (Ed.) *Music in Therapy*, published by Macmillan Publishing Co. of New York.

To be sure, one cannot write a book about music without recognizing in the strongest manner the great—and maybe the not-so-great—composers over the ages from whose pens have flowed evidence of the power of music, and confirmed why this book is necessary. As affirmation of this, daily I received (and continue to receive) inspiration and motivation from FM radio station KHFM, Albuquerque, NM, as music constantly provided a background for every step of my journey. I am forever indebted for this special gift.

Finally and foremost, I must acknowledge Bill. But how? No words are adequate to thank him for revealing a new and exciting world to me, filled with words and communication, creativity, physics, human nature, models, general semantics, existentialism, all tempered by compassion, respect, and love. Perhaps, *giving* you, the reader, the gift of words I *received* from him, is the best measure of appreciation I can express.

References

Dossey, L. (1999). *Reinventing medicine.* New York: Harper Collins.

Table of Contents

Foreword

I always said that William W. (Bill) Sears was the best problem-solver that I ever knew, he being the wisest, most logical, most reasonable, and most articulate scholarly gentleman in formal presentation or debate and/or informal conversation. His breadth of knowledge and in-depth skills were unsurpassable. In my parlance, he was the very finest thinker "on his feet" that I knew. I can now say, some 25 years after his death (d. December 1980), that Bill was unparalleled and unequalled in my 73 years of this lifetime, the best I ever knew. This book provides data toward substantiating and proving my point.

Margaret S. Sears has done an incredible(!) job of accumulating, organizing, and editing the evidence of her husband's thinking. As delineated in her "Introduction," she has brought together over a period of 25 years Bill's papers, sayings, and transcribed oral presentations, the latter of which were made without preselected notes, or if notes, very few of them. Oh, don't misunderstand, dear reader, that he had not thought concertedly about particular presentation(s) to be made! He always did. Let me give you a couple of examples.

In 1977 when I was the program chairman for the 28th Annual Conference of the National Association for Music Therapy (NAMT) held in Anaheim, California in October, Bill telephoned me in June and said that he had something he wanted to say at the conference, and told me in his usual quiet, unobtrusive, and unassuming manner. Well, knowing that whatever he needed to say would be well thought out in totality and, therefore, vitally important to the conferees, I immediately told him that I would rearrange the entire program so that he could have a general session, plenum. Those of us who attended Bill's session will never forget his message—the aesthetic and spiritual message—beyond the worded sounds, beyond the messenger (see On "Music, Mind, Education, and Human Development," Chapter 4).

The 1979 NAMT Annual Conference was held in Dallas, TX, in October. It was at a session during this conference that Bill presented his *re-vision* of his highly acclaimed "Processes in Music Therapy," one of the two lead chapters in the world's first comprehensive text published in music therapy, *Music in Therapy* (Gaston, 1968).[1] In that chapter, Bill presents

---

[1] From the dust cover, we read: "*Music in Therapy* is the first book to present a comprehensive survey of theory, research, techniques, and clinical practice in music therapy." This work of 60 contributors is organized into 39 chapters which, in turn, are grouped in 10 parts. "This book is organized around the three essential considerations for any discipline—theory, practice, and research" (p. 4). Part I has two chapters and is headed: "Foundations of Music in Therapy." Chapter 1 is "Man and Music" by E. Thayer Gaston, and Chapter 2 is "Processes in Music Therapy" by

three classification, or concepts, concerning the use of music in therapy:
experience within structure, in self-organization, and in relating to others.
As he explains, "In a sense, the several classifications are broad answers to
the question: What does music therapy offer the individual?" Within each
of the three classifications are "constructs" which attempt ". . . to define and
to limit an explicit relationship between music and the behavior of an
individual." Then, within each of the constructs are "processes," in each of
which there is an attempt ". . . to describe the manner in which the construct
affects the behavior of the individual" within the classification (p. 31).
(There are a combined total of 29 components.) These threefold aspects are
presented in the text in outlined form. This outlined, linear presentation
troubled Bill for years to come and became a process for him that had been
ongoing and all-consuming.[2] (He and I had many conversations concerning
it.) You see, Bill was the living entirety of the Processes of and in music
therapy.

In his presentation at the conference in Dallas in 1979, Bill shared
what he envisioned in music therapy Processes. He saw the 29 components
of his classifications, constructs, and processes as intertwining, helical
circles, much like electron shells circling the nucleus of an atom or
molecule, said components ever-moving . . . in, about, and among their
various parts. If the therapist could envision the whole atom/molecule and
determine the spot in the movements where it would be appropriate for the
patient, then the "spot" could be invoked in the patient-therapist session.
What Bill envisioned and conveyed was beyond the words he used, and he
knew it. How does anyone put into words that which is energized process,
especially that of music and therapy? (This reminds me of Bill once telling
me that if you name {word} it, you kill it. See?!)

The worded concepts that you will read in the Re-Vision chapter of
this current book are only the proverbial tip of the iceberg. So many of his
personal readings—so diverse and broad in their scope—and so many of his
thoughts—so profound in their relationships—were put into that Dallas

William W. Sears." I helped organize the book and was the editor of the final
manuscript in its entirety.

[2] In actual fact, Bill Sears constructed his "Processes in Music Therapy" as an
outcome of a symposium of music therapists held in Lawrence, KS in June 1964.
The purpose of the symposium was ". . . to plan a comprehensive résumé of
research and clinical practice in music therapy . . ." (1965, p. iii). The symposium
and the subsequent preparation of the résumé were made possible by a grant from
the United States Office of Education, Department of Health, Education, and
Welfare, under Public Law 531. There were 11 invited participants, including Dr.
Sears. Dr. E. Thayer Gaston of the University of Kansas was the Project Director,
and Dr. Erwin H. Schneider of Ohio State University was the Associate Director.
This résumé resulted in the published book, *Music in Therapy*, all royalties from
sales of which were donated freely to NAMT.

meeting and relayed in the current chapter. As articulate as he was, Bill struggled, suffered, and wept to relate his innermost knowing and our ultimate reality. And this knowing is better identified (in words) as *loving*.

Immediately following the conference in 1979, a symposium was held on the campus of Southern Methodist University (Dallas) where I was a professor. The inspiration for this meeting was due to an international symposium on music therapy held a year earlier (1978) in Herdecke, West Germany. Bill and I had been invited to attend that symposium, along with 32 others from 12 different countries.[3] We had been so deeply impressed and inspired at that weeklong meeting that we decided to follow through and formulate another international symposium.[4] If only you could have been there in person! Speaking of processing! The sensitivity and profundity of Bill in meeting the concerns and questions of the invited 24 music therapists from 6 different countries were extraordinary. The gentlemanly and firm guidance of Bill Sears led all of us to process creative thoughts and products none of us had ever dreamed of, never thought ourselves capable of. Margaret Sears, the editor of this book, has done a fine job of putting together notable sections of this symposium. But maybe someday the entire recordings and transcriptions will be available to you, perhaps via the Internet.

A year later, after the Dallas conference and symposium, in November 1980, Bill was to have been in Minneapolis where we again were to have an international symposium and again following the national conference of NAMT. As I was checking into the conference hotel where Bill and I were to room together, I received a telephone call from Bill. He said that he could not make it to Minneapolis, MN. So, following the conference, Clive Robbins, Roberta Kagin (Metzler), and I tried to process the symposium.[5] But, as informative as it was, this symposium was lacking. The gentle creator, the logical and reasoning one, the connector, the

---

[3] This *first* International Symposium: Music Therapy Training was held under the directorship of Dr.med. Konrad Schily and Professor Johannes Th. Eschen in Herdecke-Ruhr, Germany; October 16-21, 1978. The symposium ws co-sponsored by the Volkswagen Foundation of Germany and the Gemeinnützige Gesellschaft für angewandte wissenschaftliche Forschungen mbH.

[4] This *second* international music therapy meeting was entitled the International Symposium of the International Study Group: Theory of Music Therapy was held under the directorship of Bill Sears as Program Director and myself as Symposium Director on the campus of Southern Methodist University (SMU) in Dallas, Texas, U.S.A.; October 31-November 3, 1979. Sally Hough (Smith) was Symposium Coordinator and the transcriber of the taped recordings of the symposium. It was co-sponsored by Mr. William Jolesch and the Charles Eagle family.

[5] The Augsburg Symposium of the International Study Group: Holistic Perspectives in Music Therapy was held at Augsburg College in Minneapolis, Minnesota; November 5-6, 1980. There were 52 attendees from 3 countries.

Teacher, our Mentor, was not with us there. Six weeks later on December 13, 1980, Bill was not here.

I pray, dear reader, that you will not just read the words of this book, and won't read it straight through from cover to cover. Rather, I encourage you instead to read it as you would drink a fine wine . . . sip it by reading a paragraph or section, savor it by reflecting on it. Contemplate. Smile. Enjoy the meaning of it by consistently asking consciously and (always-present) unconsciously: Who am I? . . . to myself, to my family, to my colleagues, to . . . ? This book then will become for you what was exemplified in Bill's last recommended book (of which there were many!) to me by telephone—only a week before he passed over: *A Guide for the Perplexed* (Schumacher, 1977).

Just remember always that Bill Sears dedicated his life to you. He did what he did out of love for you, even though you may not have met him in physical form. His spherical orb of enlightened energy will always be near you and with you, as he is with me. Thanks to his wife, Margaret, we will all cherish the time well-spent in absorbing his/her wisdom. This published work will help us all to go far in experiencing and understanding the true meaning of Pythagoras (the accepted father of Western music *and* science) and his coinage of the word *philosophy*—the study of wisdom, wisdom being the insight derived from connecting the elements of experience. So, read and experience the wonders of our everlasting Mentor, Dr. William Wesley Sears. In doing so, I am sure you will agree that Bill Sears was, is, and will remain one of the great seers of our time.

Charles T. Eagle, Jr., Ph.D.
Plano, TX
September 2006

References

Gaston, E. T. (Ed). (1968). *Music in therapy*. New York: Macmillan.

Gaston, E. T. & Schneider, E. H. (Eds.), (1965). *An analysis, evaluation and selection of clinical uses of music in therapy* (Cooperative Research Project No. F-044). Lawrence, KS: The University of Kansas.

Schumacher, E. F. (1977). *A guide for the perplexed*. New York: Harper & Row.

Introduction

Bill Sears was a highly creative individual, although tangible evidence of this may not be so easily spotted. Whether it was a twirling baton or a complex philosophical question, he always looked beyond the observable, asking himself, "What more is here?" Countless other individuals can claim greater evidence of a creative nature, but, I daresay none have been less prejudicial or judgmental, or expected less of a payoff. Speak the words "baton twirling" and one automatically titters, thinking only of shapely young women dressed in scanty, spangly costumes, leaping high in the air in the process of executing a high toss. Bill saw much more. He saw it as a marriage between the body and a stick which required experimentation to discover what secrets were locked in that union. During his twirling days he never executed the same routine twice because in the process of performing it he discovered something new that previously had gone unnoticed. So, it was back to the drawing board in an attempt to understand what new concept that observation could produce.

It was no accident that Bill chose the body's muscular system for both his master's thesis and doctoral dissertation. Many years of observing and physically experiencing his own muscular actions while twirling convinced him that the muscular system played a much larger role in man's nature than generally had been attributed to it. Even more important was the linkage between muscles and music. "What more is here?"

Our house was brimming over with strange-looking homemade mechanical contrivances, which, no doubt, served some purpose in Bill's creative world, but to my mind were lacking in aesthetic or pragmatic appeal. He frequently engaged guests in author Edward de Bono type creative parlor tricks, carrying these also into the classroom. "What if . . ." time and time again prefaced his remarks in the classroom, lecture hall, and casual conversation. He posed more questions than answers, a situation that created confusion for anyone—particularly students—who believed that learning consisted primarily of obtaining answers to questions, and that in those answers security could be found. Rarely did he present the therapist or the teacher with concrete techniques or recipes to follow in the clinic or the classroom. Instead, he offered numerous thinking tools—models and ideas which would open the door of individual awareness to the process. This style is apparent in the present work, for he places more emphasis on challenging the reader to interject his/her personal interpretations on issues than offering his (Sears') opinion. His philosophy of learning was not unique, by any means, but his non-pedagogical approach often made it seem so.

It was this pervasive questioning that in large measure prevented Bill from writing. He admitted as much in Anaheim, CA at the outset of his 1977 National Association for Music Therapy conference presentation (see On "Music, Mind, Education, and Human Development," Chapter 4) when he confessed, "I have often been told that I should write, that I have important things to say. Writing, however, is for me most difficult." Each idea raised more questions and doubts in his mind, and, for whatever other reasons, stayed his pen. Of course, he enjoyed indulging in the questioning. It was much more gratifying than the arduous task of writing scholarly papers. This is not to say he wrote not at all; but, the preponderance of his message was embodied in the verbal environment of the classroom and informal exchange with colleagues.

Upon his death I set about to locate what tangible evidence remained of his message. Because Bill rarely wrote his speeches and lectures, what I located came from tape recordings, lecture handouts, rough drafts of speeches, notes, and recollections—both my own and others. This book is the culmination of that search. In some ways it is a walk through Bill Sears' life. Each chapter reveals what was concerning him at that particular time of his life. Some themes recur over and over while others make only a brief appearance. The most striking of the former is the "Processes in Music Therapy."

Sears' first known speech of record about the Processes was presented at the 1963 NAMT conference in Bloomington, IN. The title was "Dynamic Processes in Music Therapy." He said, "there are many dynamics in the therapeutic relationship, and they are closely related to our conceptual processes—the way we see things. Now it probably makes no difference which school of thought we adopt, . . . [for] these are conceptual ideas—[merely] a framework of thought . . . . Too many times our own dynamic processes say that this particular concept is what is happening rather than the behavior" (Sears, 1963, p. 3). Five years later, the Processes constituted Bill's contribution to the text *Music in Therapy* (Sears, 1968), Chapter 1 herein. Some 11 years still later, they continued to consume his attention, and a revision of the 1968 product appeared in 1979 at the NAMT conference in Dallas. This revision, Chapter 2, is the centerpiece of the present work.

Editing from an oral delivery to the printed page presents its own unique problems and dangers, for, in some ways, the two forms of communication are alien to each other. The problem I encountered was even more overwhelming since Bill left no written record of his words. The challenge before me was to convert an informal verbal style to a formal written one, employing absolutely minimal editing. It takes much courage and more than a bit of arrogance to change the words of another, especially when that other does not have the benefit of redress. In defense of these charges I level against myself, I relied heavily on 30 years' discussion and debate and my knowledge of the man. Of equal or greater importance, Charles T. Eagle, Bill's long-time colleague and special friend, provided his own special expertise by reading and critiquing the complete manuscript. He was present when many of the presentations were made, and had discussed them and untold other ideas in depth with Bill.

Organizing the various presentations into a logical and sequential order posed no small task for me. Originally, a chronological sequence was adopted, the rationale being that such a system displayed a perceived evolution in Bill's thinking processes, which could be found in many of the papers. However, this arrangement took on the appearance of a memoir rather than a concept-based text. Additionally, the degree of ideational duplication was too great to justify fusion into a single work. Thus, it was determined after 27 publisher rejections of the first effort, followed by a hiatus of over 15 years, that in order to create a cohesive collection of Bill's thinking, reorganization and removal of repetitious subject matter was necessary. There followed extensive shifting, juggling, and deleting, and eventually the present work emerged. I literally cut apart the original draft, created a keyword list, and spread piles of the text by keyword on my study floor. (And would you believe, my dogs never disturbed them!) The Introduction to each chapter explains its origin and the extent of editing and rearranging required.

Bill believed so unequivocally in models, that he devoted no fewer than three major papers to the subject. Two of these have been consolidated as Chapter 3, and retitled, "Models for Thinking." The third, which was presented a year later, could not be located. One can only speculate how many new models he included, and how many additional ways he discovered of using those included in the earlier presentations. His obsession with models can be traced in part to a Christmas gift he received a number of years ago. It was the mind puzzle, *Hexed*. This seemingly uncomplicated "game" consists of 12 pieces, each having a different geometrical shape, which when fitted together properly form a rectangle. Of course, the solution is much more difficult than it appears at first glance. He took the puzzle to school after the Christmas break, and for ever after it served as a significant educational tool which was utilized many times over. Thus, it seems fitting that *Hexed*, the puzzle which was so central to Bill's life and teaching, should introduce the reader to thinking models in Chapter 3.

The title for Chapter 4, "On Music, Mind, Education, and Human Development," was inspired by J. T. Fraser's seminal text, *Of Time, Passion, and Knowledge*. That chapter title eloquently, yet succinctly, expresses Bill's message better than any attempted annotation. This NAMT presentation at Anaheim, CA was possibly Bill's most introspective, eclectic, and philosophical public address, and thus its message may extend further afield than would be expected in a book about music therapy. However, although his audience was primarily music therapists, his message was meant for any inquiring human beings who often wonder, "What more is here?"

At this point in the original manuscript, the content began to be repetitious, and needed extensive reworking. The principal question I raised was: What major themes could be found spread throughout the remaining chapters expressing Bill's philosophy? Unquestionably, "The Influence of Music on Behavior," Chapter 5, was one such theme. It is the basic foundation upon which the music therapy discipline rests, yet all too often the literature is silent about it. E. Thayer Gaston is often quoted in response to the question, "Whatever happened to the influence of music on behavior?" As I recollect the numerous discussions with colleagues about this weighty topic, it was Charles Eagle who first raised the question, at least in my presence.

A section devoted to "time" was mandatory. Thus, it was determined that in order to give it the attention warranted, much of what Sears had to say about this illusory, incomprehensible concept [or is "time" an entity, an essence, or something else? Immediately I had a conundrum in an effort to find the proper grammatical descriptor for "time." Even Fraser, after the thousands of pages he has written about "time," was of little help. As with me, his favored terms appeared to be "concept" and "entity." No assistance was found in the one-and-a-half long columns *Webster's (3rd) International Dictionary* nor the 34 categories *The Original Roget's Thesaurus* devoted to "time".] needed to be consolidated rather than sprinkled throughout all the chapters. "Time, the Servant of Music," Chapter 6, is the result of that amalgamation.

"Semantic and Existential Implications for Music Therapy," Chapter 7, is not a compilation as are the previous three chapters, but instead, a largely complete set of notes for a conference lecture. The contents could easily be perceived as a basic introduction to the fields of general semantics and existential psychology. If, indeed, these notes represent the speech given at the 1962 Great Lakes (NAMT) Regional conference, is anyone still around who attended?

One paper which is not included as such in this text, although highly significant, came from the second music therapy international symposium held in 1979 at Southern Methodist University, Dallas, TX. (The first symposium occurred the previous year in Herdecke, Germany.) I carefully perused the transcription and cogitated endlessly, trying to place the symposium discussion, which Bill led, into the present work, but could not find a "fit." The obvious reason was not that the symposium material was beyond the ken of this work, but rather the large amount of duplication existing with parts of other papers, which *are* included herein. One prime example is the handouts of numerous models Bill distributed to and discussed with the group, most of which are in Chapter 3, "Models for Thinking." The solution I reached was to fold related symposium discussion into different chapters.

There were other reasons to omit the complete symposium. Most compelling was the desire of the organizers to publish the proceedings of both international gatherings as a vehicle to advance the knowledge of music therapy worldwide. Thus, I thought that it would be inappropriate to trade on that right. Most assuredly, the symposium record deserves its own showcase, not a merging with other events and ideas. However, although the symposium papers are missing from this text, much of what happened those four days is woven into several of the chapters, and contributed significantly to the overall meaningfulness of this volume.

The references at the end of each chapter contain a broad mixture of topics and authors Bill consulted to reinforce his message. When commenting about J. Samuel Bois' work, *The Art of Awareness*, which is cited in "Models for Thinking and Time, the Servant of Music," Sears said, "If I were to choose a single book that may put it all together for me, *The Art of Awareness* is probably the one. So, if you want to know me, read the books I read." Keep this in mind when you read his commentary on Bois' theories. Later in that same lecture (second music therapy international symposium), he said, "You think you know the people with whom you interact regularly, but if you want to verify your impressions, examine the books they talk about. You will discover all kinds of secrets about me from my books by noting where I scribble in them, where I don't, what I underline—sometimes with an objectionable comment. An insightful exercise you may wish to engage in is to pen your remarks in the margins of the books you read, then criticize your remarks. An interesting study would be to analyze the marked music scores of orchestral conductors." I took Bill at his word literally as I edited his discourses, leafing through many of his books for insightful margin notes. I was not disappointed.

Repeatedly, Bill emphasized that those he was addressing should take his discussion points further, placing their own personal stamp on them. About the Processes, he said they are "not finished today, and I hope [they] never will be." (see "Re-Vision and Expansion of Processes in Music Therapy," Chapter 2, p. 22). He juxtaposed authors with opposing views beside one another, mentioning many but endorsing few (maybe none). That is not to say he did not revere certain great thinkers. He did, of course, but he was more inclined to share his admiration of these persons than to subscribe to their views.

As my work progressed, I could not refrain from wondering, and subsequently investigating, what more had come from the pens of the authors Bill cited in the intervening years since he died. I discovered valuable information that I believed complemented Bill's message. It is here that I exercised some license—possibly beyond what some might find acceptable—by appending new material I believed was pertinent to the original but written after 1980. In a manner of speaking, I was following Bill's advice to explore "what more is here."

During this laborious and exacting re-birthing process of "Bill's Book," I received an e-mail from Roberta Kagin who knew of my project. She described several unsettling dreams she had about the Processes, primarily about their unpublished status. "I worry a lot," Roberta wrote, "that Bill's contributions . . . will always [be] set in concrete in Chapter 2 [Gaston's *Music in Therapy* (1968)] unless something else is published that will show his depth of theory . . . . There is so much more that he had to say to us." If I had been dispirited or even worse—apathetic—before, Roberta's comments jolted me from that state to resume the quest I had temporarily abandoned.

Roberta had even more to say later as I was writing this Introduction and sought her permission to quote her e-mail message. Expanding on the earlier commentary, she said, "When read from the standpoint of the multiplicity of connecting threads and patterns of the original "Processes in Music Therapy" (Sears, 1968), Dr. Sears' "Re-Vision of the Processes in Music Therapy" form a spiral of awareness of the unique and influential power of music to reach into the potential of one's humanness. The original Processes (Sears, 1968, Chap. 2) and Dr. E. Thayer Gaston's eight "fundamental considerations of man in relation to music" (Gaston, 1968, Chap. 1, pp. 21–27), which comprise "Foundations of Music in Therapy, Part I" in *Music in Therapy*, presented a crucial new dimension for the modern academic understanding of the function of music. These writings formed the foundation for the early music therapy degrees, first established in the United States in the 1940s. Selected colleges and universities continue to consider them the essential cornerstones on which the field of music therapy was built and continues to evolve."

In the original manuscript there was a chapter entitled, "Commentary by Bill." It contained numerous notes covering a myriad of topics which Bill had scribbled in the margins of books (as I mentioned earlier), tucked in drawers, file folders, and even pants pockets. Many, but not all, have been incorporated into this work. Yet there are a few residuals which I believe cannot end up where I found them. Thus, the following "commentary by Bill" deserve to be mentioned.]

> "Education professors talk[ed] about developing the *whole* child. The trouble is, the 'hole' is the one we put him in."
> "Good education is just preventive therapy."

"Yes, [behavior modification] works, but so does the atom bomb!"
"We compromise our humanity, in a sense, every time we adopt a system that is not part of us and which we cannot use comfortably."

A final word about the book *in toto*. It offers few, if any solutions. It presents more questions than answers. At times, the reader is left in midair, anticipating, but never receiving a full explanation. Yet, of most significance, throughout is displayed a variety of concepts, notions—many sides of an argument, actually—about which one can ruminate. Bill often gives us only a glimpse from the doorway, if you will, of what lies beyond—at the leading edge. He takes us to the leading edge and stops! We will have to go through the door to the edge alone, and then only after we have struggled individually to find the knowledge and understanding that will permit us entrance. Karl Pribram put it well by claiming that if you are somewhere on the leading edge, you cannot explain everything. "If you knew all about it, it wouldn't be the leading edge" (Pribram, 1982, p. 20). Thus, respected reader, I hope this book will help you on your own personal journey to the leading edge, and that you will believe Bill when he said,

"To be always continued, but not by me."

Margaret S. Sears
Santa Fe, NM

References

Dutch, R. A. (Ed.). (1965). *The original Roget's thesaurus of English words and phrases*. New York: St. Martin's Press.

Ferguson, M. (1982). Karl Pribram's changing reality. In K. Wilber (Ed.), *The holographic paradigm*. Boulder, CO: Shambhala.

Gaston, E. T. (Ed.). (1968). *Music in therapy*. New York: Macmillan.

Gaston, E. T. (1968). Music and man. In E. T. Gaston (Ed.), *Music in therapy*. New York: Macmillan.

Sears, W. W. (1963). *Dynamic processes in music therapy*. Paper presented at the National Association for Music Therapy conference, Bloomington, IN.

Sears. W. W. (1968). Processes in music therapy. In E. T. Gaston (Ed.), *Music in therapy*. New York: Macmillan.

Webster's third new international dictionary. (1961). Springfield, MA: G. & C. Merriam.

Chapter 1

Processes in Music Therapy

Editor's Introduction

A "Re-vision and Expansion of Processes in Music Therapy," Chapter 2, being the centerpiece of the present work, begs the question, "What is the original 'vision' upon which that chapter is based?" The answer: this opening chapter, "Processes in Music Therapy," Chapter 2 from E. Thayer Gaston (Ed.). *Music in Therapy*. New York: Macmillan, 1968. Therefore, it was determined that to enhance the reader's understanding of the full meaning of the processes in music therapy, the original Processes and the "re-vision" should be placed alongside one another. Even more to the point, many persons may not be familiar with Gaston's text. (Some were not even born when it was published!) Further, a comparison of the two should help the reader gain insight into the developmental—actually evolutionary—process which resulted in the latter.

More than 14 years lapsed from when the Processes first appeared in print in Gaston and Schneider's (1965) *Analysis, Evaluation, and Selection of Clinical Uses of Music in Therapy*, a grant-supported work which was the precursor to *Music in Therapy* (see Chapter 2 References for complete citation) and the Dallas presentation in 1979. During that hiatus, Sears had ample time to allow new concepts to evolve which invigorated and strengthened the Processes, giving them greater clarity and an added dimension.

[Prelude to the Processes]

Music therapy is closely related to the behavioral sciences because it often concerns musically elicited behavior in therapeutic situations. Because music therapy is a very young discipline, much of its data and knowledge have been obtained through empirical observation, and sometimes the data are not as factual and well organized as they should be. Nevertheless, modern music therapy seeks to establish itself on acceptable scientific observation.

To describe music therapy as being closely related to behavioral science should not be thought presumptuous. Such a relationship implies an orientation and method of approach to verified knowledge; it does not declare that all, or even most, is known. The scientific approach does not negate the presently mysterious beauty of music. When this beauty is gone, there is no reason for music. It seems the nature of man to seek organization, classification, and description until a system emerges. This is the case in all sciences, and music therapy is no exception. To present such a system, even if incomplete, is the purpose of this writing. It will classify and describe processes in music therapy. The system can be characterized as behavioral, logical, and psychological.

Specific discussion of the music therapist has been omitted, although his presence is implied. This omission does not mean that his role is unimportant. Because a therapist is a common factor in most therapeutic situations, his adequacy as a therapist in the broad sense is, of course, related to successful therapy. The intent here, however, is to help him be more proficient as a *music* therapist by giving him a better theoretical understanding of the function of music in therapy. Furthermore, this discussion of processes in music therapy does not intend to tell the music therapist what to do. "What to do" is left to the therapist and should be based on his understanding of the theory and practice necessary to achieve the goals of treatment.

No attempt is made here to describe how music or music therapists can be used in combination with other therapeutic approaches. This does not imply that music therapy is considered a cure-all or that it cannot be used with other media. It signifies only that consideration of combined therapeutic approaches is beyond the scope of this discussion.

Of most importance in any therapeutic situation is the person receiving therapy. Only through the individual's behavior, and changes therein, can the success of a therapeutic endeavor be seen. Thus, behavioral descriptions, insofar as possible, receive major consideration. The terms are defined and used in a logical and consistent manner. This should permit better communication among the individuals concerned. Finally, the classifications and descriptions are consistent with pertinent and accepted psychological principles and theories. No attempt is made, however, to express the classifications and descriptions in the terminology of any particular psychiatric or psychotherapeutic school of thought. Rather, a definite attempt is made to express them free of such connections, to express them as specifics, properly a part of music therapy. This is done not to create the impression of a new school of thought nor to claim any special status for music therapy, but to permit the fitting of what music therapy has to offer into various orientations.

Classification, as used here, signifies a general idea, a broad concept or category, concerning the use of music in therapy. In a sense, the several classifications are broad answers to the question: What does music therapy offer the individual? A *construct* attempts to propose formally, to define and to limit, an explicit relationship between music and the behavior of an individual. The *process* then attempts to describe the manner in which the construct affects the behavior of the individual.

The various classifications and constructs with their processes are not mutually exclusive. In any given therapeutic situation, several, or all, may be operating; however, the various exemplifications were deemed both significant and necessary to permit their delineation and to identify bases for specific therapeutic action.

In most cases, only the word "music" has been used in reference to musical situations, although it may have any of four designations: (1) the music itself; (2) listening to music; (3) having music in the environment; and (4) the making of music. The processes should permit the reader to determine which of the four is meant. Furthermore, the use of the single term, music, may lead some readers to think more deeply about the application of a given construct to situations other than the obvious, thus expanding the function of the construct. The three classifications that underlie the constructs and processes of music therapy are (1) experience within structure, (2) experience in self-organization, and (3) experience in relating to others.[*]

The words used to phrase the classifications were chosen purposely and carefully. Each classification is defined later; however, at this point, the word *experience* should be made clear. For most persons, this word signifies events through which one has lived. Experience, however, may also designate the actual living through, or undergoing, of events in the present. Furthermore, it can be used either as a noun or a transitive verb—the gerund and the present participle being "experiencing." In a basic sense, *music therapy offers the individual the experiencing of events in certain ways; the processes attempt to define those ways of experiencing.*

Although past experiences of the individual may serve as a basis (often a very important one) for organizing the therapeutic situation, that situation always begins in the present and goes into the future. No therapist

---

[*] At first, five classifications were formulated: (1) gratification, (2) structured experience, (3) environment conducive to recovery, (4) relationships, and (5) diagnosis and evaluation. After further analysis of the classifications, only three were considered necessary. In all phases of the use of music in therapy, "diagnosis and evaluation" should be constant activities. The principles originally placed under that classification would also logically fall under "structured experience." Somewhat similarly, "environment conducive to recovery" implies a definite structure, and "relationships," although not strictly equivalent to, might be considered as, socializing experience. Temporarily, the three classifications became structured experience, gratifying experience, and socializing experience. Gratifying and socializing, however, are commonly used terms and, in part, are associated with certain psychiatric and psychotherapeutic schools of thought. To avoid misinterpretations that might arise from the use of the more common terms and because their meanings were not strictly what was desired, the terms *self-organizing experience* and *other-relating experience*, to be defined later, were selected.

can change the past experiences of the individual, but he can organize a *present* situation so that the *effect of the past* is altered for a more adequate *future*. It is in this sense—that of the present going into the future—that the word "experience" has been selected for use.

Even though all the classifications might be considered equally well as experience within structure, the term *structure* has been reserved for the first classification in order to emphasize the uniqueness of music—the structure demanding experiencing is inherent in the music. The order of terms in the adopted classifications is important and indicative. A natural order is evident in the progression—an individual must be aware of or have some structure before an experience can become his or become organized. Also, the individual must have organization (possibly in his own version, when viewed by another individual) before he will use the experience externally or overtly. Assuming this order, are there similar orders by which to express the constructs under each classification? If so, on what bases? Three such bases seemed appropriate.

One possible order was founded on the continuum from how much of an individual's behavior is required *by the music itself* to how much is required *by the situation* in which music is used. Phrased in another way, how much control of behavior is demanded by the music and how much by the therapist's manipulation of the environment? (This was thought to apply to the major classifications, also.) A second basis was the consideration of the directness with which the behavior might be observed—again a kind of continuum, directly observable behavior to inferred behavior, for example, "He played his note on time" to "He looks like the music made him sad." One further basis seemed logical: Could the behavior be graded on a continuum from simple (almost reflex or conditioned response) to complex (involving integration of several or many simple responses), for example, from just beating a drum to beating it *appropriately* so that others might play or dance with the beat?

The classifications and constructs are presented in outline form, both for convenience and to show the influence on their development of the three orders or bases described.

A. Experience within structure
  1. Music demands time-ordered behavior.
     a. Music demands reality-ordered behavior.
     b. Music demands immediately and continuously objectified behavior.
  2. Music permits ability-ordered behavior.
     a. Music permits ordering of behavior according to physical response levels.

    b. Music permits ordering of behavior according to psychological response levels.
3. Music evokes affectively ordered behavior.
4. Music provokes sensory-elaborated behavior.
    a. Music demands increased sensory usage and discrimination.
    b. Music may elicit extramusical ideas and associations.

B. Experience in self-organization
1. Music provides for self-expression.
2. Music provides compensatory endeavors for the handicapped individual.
3. Music provides opportunities for socially acceptable reward and nonreward.
4. Music provides for the enhancement of pride in self.
    a. Music provides for successful experiences.
    b. Music provides for feeling needed by others.
    c. Music provides for enhancement of esteem by others.

C. Experience in relating to others
1. Music provides means by which self-expression is socially acceptable.
2. Music provides opportunity for individual choice of response in groups.
3. Music provides opportunities for acceptance of responsibility to self and others.
    a. Music provides for developing self-directed behavior.
    b. Music provides for developing other-directed behavior.
4. Music enhances verbal and nonverbal social interaction and communication.
5. Music provides for experiencing cooperation and competition in socially acceptable forms.
6. Music provides entertainment and recreation necessary to the general therapeutic environment.
7. Music provides for learning realistic social skills and personal behavior patterns acceptable in institutional and community peer groups.

Experience Within Structure

Experience within structure refers to those behaviors of an individual that are required by and are inherent in musical experience. Even though a therapist must prepare the experience for the individual, the mere commitment to the experience places the individual in a situation where his (future) behavior is determined primarily by musical factors and not by other factors or persons in his environment. The commitment to the structured experience may be only temporary, for the duration of the music or some part of it. This, however does not negate the possible continued influence of the music on the individual; it refers mainly to the immediately observable behavior of the individual. Furthermore, music is not considered impersonal. (The meaning, or importance, of music to the individual belongs in the next classification, experience in self-organization.) The focus of concern, here, is on the musically structured experience and on the behavior required by that structure. The motivation for this experience tends to be an intrinsic quality of the music, which carries its own persuasion for behavior.

At this level, the individual is involved in coming to terms and getting along with a part of his environment, a musical part in this case. He may be led to understand and respect certain laws of the environment, the gaining of such understanding and respect possibly made easier because the demands come from the music. His awareness of structures as useful and necessary may take on an elaboration through the meaningful and objective connecting of symbols and referents. Along with this elaboration, the individual is required to expand his self, to discover some of his own potentialities, and to govern himself—facets of development leading to the next level, experience in self-organization.

Major goals in therapy are to lengthen the temporal commitment (objectively measurable), to vary the commitment (objectively describable), and to stimulate an awareness (inferred from behavior and directly related to the next level) of the benefits derived thereby.

Music Demands Time-ordered Behavior

The unique structure of music—it exists only through time—requires the individual to commit himself to the experience moment by moment. Except for relatively minute deviations, music (whether an entire piece or merely a measure or phrase in repeated practice) cannot be interrupted without losing its intent. Participation in music is not ordinarily achieved by a note a day. Once begun, music must be continued without interruption in order that a completed idea or expression may result; regardless of its length or complexity or the type and degree of skill it requires, the music must be carried through in its time order.

The necessity for moment-to-moment commitment by the individual rests in the music itself and does not derive from any other part of his environment. The extent and rapidity of the commitment can be adjusted to the individual by an appropriate selection of the level of skill required, the length and complexity of the music, and the specific responses required, including the number of responses per unit of time.

Time order, as conceived here, is a broader concept than rhythm. On the most elementary level, it involves the sequence of sounds and no sounds. On other levels, it concerns not only the making of sounds at the correct times (rhythm), but also the correct sounds (pitches), the correct emphases or stresses of those sounds (dynamics), the accuracy in making several sounds together (harmony and ensemble), and the organization of other kinds of sounds (timbre). Regardless of the organizations in music, the underlying factor is time order.

This construct is considered fundamental to all the other constructs. It might be called the working principle. Building on the time-ordered structure inherent in music, the skillful therapist can involve the individual in any of the relationships defined by the other constructs. An individual develops through time; music develops through time—uniquely, the tempos of life and music are quite comparable, possibly even congruent.

This construct also emphasizes the uniqueness of music when contrasted with other approaches used in therapy. Even though all experiences have beginnings and go into the future, the time order of music requires the individual to structure his behavior in, relatively, the most minute and continuous manner. No other form of human behavior both demands and depends so completely on strict adherence to time-ordered structure.

MUSIC DEMANDS REALITY-ORDERED BEHAVIOR. Once the individual is committed to music, his behavior becomes reality ordered. Music involves reality orientations in many forms and on such levels as the situation requires—responses to, for example, aural stimuli, musical and verbal; instruments; musical notation; conductor's or therapist's directions; and the individual's own body and its parts. The individual's responses can be judged for their appropriateness to the "real" stimuli, stimuli built on the time-ordered necessities of a given musical situation and established in the individual's environment by the therapist.

A question concerning the place of free improvisation and the possibility that it would not necessarily be reality ordered might be raised here. (Improvisation is included in the next classification, experience in self-organization.) Concern is for the individual's evidenced behavior and not for what the music means to him. Improvising implies doing something that is meaningful to the person doing the improvising. The pursuit of meaning in music is personal and internal. The ability to improvise, at least meaningfully for others, demands a background of structured experiences that permits the improvisation to take place. Thus, at this level and within the meaning and intent here, the question is premature.

MUSIC DEMANDS IMMEDIATELY AND CONTINUOUSLY OBJECTIFIED BEHAVIOR. Once committed to the music, the individual's behavior is no longer subjective, but becomes immediately observable or "objectified." The musical appropriateness of the behavior must always be judged with reference to the ability of the individual. Furthermore, his behavior is continuously objectified and observable, requiring attention to the music through the duration of the musical experience, even if attention fluctuates.

Because the time order of music is continuous, the individual's responses must be continuous; and because the individual's responses are continuous, the appropriateness of his responses are immediately observable, moment by moment.

Music Permits Ability-ordered Behavior

The behavioral requirements in music are uniquely adaptable to the individual's operational levels and capacities. Musical behaviors, the specific functionings of the individual in specific musical situations, range from the simple to the complex, from the awareness or performance of a simple rhythmic beat to the awareness or performance of a highly complex musical structure. Behaviors ranging from simple to complex may coexist among several individuals, as in group performance where the behavioral requirements of one musical part are of a more simple nature, such as beating the bass drum, than those of another part, such as playing the melody on a trumpet. Also, especially desired musical experiences, such as playing a certain piece, can be modified or adapted (rearranged) to fit the capabilities of each individual.

MUSIC PERMITS ORDERING OF BEHAVIOR ACCORDING TO PHYSICAL RESPONSE LEVELS. Required musical behavior can be adapted to the physical capacities and operational levels of the individual. The physically handicapped can be helped to make music by the use of special devices, such as especially designed mouthpieces or prostheses. Modifications of the traditional positions for playing certain instruments, such as placing a bass drum on its side or preparing a special stand for an instrument, can be made to permit the use of the individual's movement capabilities. The variety of physical movements used in playing musical instruments or in singing offers a wide range for structuring needed muscular movements. The attainment of gratifying musical ends usually makes such exercises more acceptable to the individual.

MUSIC PERMITS ORDERING OF BEHAVIOR ACCORDING TO PSYCHOLOGICAL RESPONSE LEVELS. Required musical behavior can be adapted to psychological capacities and operational levels. The psychological levels may have several bases: (1) mood—such as sad to happy, depressed to manic; (2) motivation—low to high desire to achieve; (3) intellect—mentally retarded to gifted; or (4) levels of musical knowledge. Partly through the motivation intrinsic to music and partly through the appropriate structure provided by the therapist, the individual can either be moved from a less desirable to a more desirable psychological level or have the requirements of the activity suited and paced appropriately to his capabilities, as the case may be.

Music Evokes Affectively-ordered Behavior

The general behavior of groups can be controlled, or at least influenced, by appropriately chosen music. Slow tempos, smooth (legato) lines, simple harmonies, and little dynamic change are characteristic of music that tends to reduce or sedate physical activity and, possibly, to enhance the contemplative activity of individuals; fast tempos, detached (staccato) lines, complex and dissonant harmonies, and abrupt dynamic changes tend to increase or stimulate physical activity and, possibly, to reduce mental activity. Given a knowledgeable use of music, the desired result is usually achieved with groups; prediction is less sure when dealing with an individual because of the possible unique associations he may have with the particular music or with music in general. These associations in themselves can be significant.

Music Provokes Sensory-elaborated Behavior

Sensory stimulation and resulting awareness have been shown to be human needs. Participation in music offers unique sensory experiences ranging from just perceptible responses on the neuromuscular level to the highest level of human behavior—intellectual mediation and contemplation—all of which are essential to esthetic experience. Furthermore, both initiation and recall of experiences involving sight, sound, odors, tactile sensations, and so on, can be evoked by music. Experiences such as the smell of rosin on the bow; the tactile sensation of vibration; and the auditory and visual awareness of concerted efforts, such as identical phrasing, bowing by stringed-instrument players, and breathing by wind-instrument players, offer an elaborate world of sensations.

MUSIC DEMANDS INCREASED SENSORY USAGE AND DISCRIMINATION. Involvement in music requires the individual both to become more aware of and to refine his use of sensory data in a great variety of forms. Not only must he increase his auditory discrimination of pitch, volume, rhythmic, and quality differences, he also must bring into use and refine all other sensory modalities: sight, for reading symbols, responding to visual instructions, and seeing where different sounds come from; touch, for contacting the instrument in what are sometimes very delicate ways and for receiving temperature sensations from different instruments and their parts; proprioception, for learning to breathe correctly, producing correct vocal sounds, and controlling body parts; and smell and taste, which, although less describable, are nonetheless involved. Music significantly demands the integrated use of several or all of these sensory modalities at any given time within the musical experience.

MUSIC MAY ELICIT EXTRAMUSICAL IDEAS AND ASSOCIATIONS., Music may often bring about certain pictures or ideas. When the individual's ideas fall outside the "normal," his differences may reveal significant insights into his particular structuring of his world. Such insights have been used as the basis of several projective tests and also in psychotherapy. In certain cases, the association-provoking quality of music can be used to reinstate or remind the individual of healthy forms of behavior, including ideas.

Experience in Self-Organization

Experience in self-organization concerns inner responses that may only be inferred from behavior, and has to do with a person's attitudes, interests, values, and appreciations, with his meaning to himself. It includes most, if not all, of what has been commonly termed gratification and also the strictly personal factors in the esthetic experience. (Of concern here is not only gratification, but also the fact that nearly all people like some kind of music very much.)

At this level, the individual may come to discover what he really is— to find his own ways of living, of valuing and appreciating himself as an individual with potentialities. He may come to discover that these potentialities have sufficient meaning to himself to be used for experience in relating to others.

A common goal in therapy is to structure experiences (objectively describable) so that the individual receives the satisfactions (inferred) necessary for him to seek more such experiences (objectively measurable), and to see that such experiences lend themselves to the maintenance of better adjustment (objectively describable) with his environment.

Music Provides for Self-Expression

Whenever choice by an individual is involved, his behavior is a reflection of his self-expressive needs. These needs, although not in themselves directly observable, may give rise to consistent patterns of behavior. Such patterns of behavior can become the bases for structuring activities in which the person will be involved, in making possible or impossible (or at least limiting) the continuance of certain behaviors. The adaptability of music provides many avenues for self-expression in performance and listening; they range from random to complex and highly organized. Such a wide range also offers many socially acceptable ways of expressing negative feelings, energetic behavior, and closeness, any of which may reduce the need for expression in more overt, unacceptable forms. The movement from random expression to organized, meaningful expression is the goal.

Music Provides Compensatory Endeavors for the Handicapped Individual

By being helped to accomplish in music some of the same things that his "normal" counterpart does, the handicapped individual may be led to a healthy acceptance of his limitations. He may come to place his handicap in perspective, as a limitation only of his means, as only one aspect of himself, rather than his whole person.

Music Provides Opportunities for Socially Acceptable Reward and Nonreward

When appropriately structured, musical activities may carry an inherent pleasure found in the performance itself. The individual may, realistically, receive commendation where indicated for musical and/or treatment purposes; or commendation may be withheld. The adaptability of music provides many opportunities for rewards, ranging from immediate to long term. In music, it is generally the performance that receives negative criticism, not the individual. In this way, the criticism need not become rejection.

Music Provides for the Enhancement of Pride in Self

Positive learning experiences usually enhance an individual's feelings of worth. A foreseeable product or result often serves as its own stimulus to learning. The adaptability of music to learning, on many levels of required ability, makes it uniquely versatile for structuring situations leading to feelings of pride. The individual is confronted with objective evidence concerning the relationship of effort spent and goal achieved.

MUSIC PROVIDES FOR SUCCESSFUL EXPERIENCES. The individual may choose, or have arranged for him, a level of musical participation almost certain to ensure success. Careful guidance of the activity and the wide range of experiences offered by music make this possible. The permissive atmosphere of most musical group activities provides a continuum of opportunities for successful experience, ranging from mere presence within a group to a position of prominence.

MUSIC PROVIDES FOR FEELING NEEDED BY OTHERS. Successful performance normally leads to enhancement of self-esteem. The feeling of being needed by others, of giving the self to an important pursuit, and of achievement, may be gained through especially structured musical situations. Situations specifically structured toward this end (and under the next construct) provide necessary support for the individual to commit himself voluntarily to experiences in relating to others.

MUSIC PROVIDES FOR ENHANCEMENT OF ESTEEM BY OTHERS. A person who shares successful musical experiences with others or contributes to the success of others through a supporting role normally receives the esteem of others. Due commendation can be given and positions of leadership can be arranged in structured musical situations.

Experience in Relating to Others

Experience in relating to others deals with the behavior of the individual in relation to other individuals, singly or in groups. Music provides experiences for persons as group members. The music is the reason for being together; the individual need not participate in the group except as a musician, and he is usually accepted when doing so. Ensemble music, however, requires the individual to subordinate his own interests to those of the group if music is to result; this demand, although possibly enforced by another person, objectively derives from the music and not from the other person. Such experiences, considerately arranged, may support the individual in his feeling of being needed by others—to gain identity in a whole (group) larger than himself.

Also at this level, and possibly of greatest importance, the individual is enabled to assess his identity. *Only by self-comparison with the group can the individual become aware of his identity and his accomplishments.* This comparison, if appropriately provided, may stimulate the individual to further accomplishment; if inappropriately provided, the experience may lead to a rejection of, or at least reduced desire for, similar experiences. Thus, caution must be exercised by the therapist.

The goal is to increase the size of the group in which the individual can successfully interact (objectively measurable and describable); to increase range and flexibility of his behavior in those interactions (objectively describable); and to provide experiences that will help him relate to noninstitutional life (objectively describable).

Music Provides Means by Which Self-Expression Is Socially Acceptable

Music provides a wide range of emotional expression. Positive, as well as negative, feelings for others can be expressed through music, and social acceptance is usually forthcoming or at least permitted. Ways to achieve and excel through superior performance are abundantly provided and accepted in music. Dance activities permit a closeness to other individuals not normally possible in a different situation. Both transitory and continuing feelings are expressible in music.

Music Provides Opportunity for Individual Choice of Response in Groups

Optimum performance of each individual in a musical group is desirable. However, the individual may wish to choose his own level of response. Because it is desirable for the patient to *wish* to make choices, opportunity to do so must be provided. Freedom to choose is sometimes more important than the choice.

Music Provides Opportunities for Acceptance of Responsibility to Self and Others

Music provides many opportunities for the individual to accept responsibility. His arrival on time for lessons or other activities or his participation as an important member of a group requires him to be responsible to others. Music may be his reason, at first, for accepting responsibility, but extension to acceptance in general is the goal.

MUSIC PROVIDES FOR DEVELOPING SELF-DIRECTED BEHAVIOR. The wide range of experiences and levels of achievement offered in music permits the individual a variety of choice in personal goals. Once a choice has been made, the individual must initiate and maintain the practice required to reach the goal. Although the situation may be structured to assist the individual in attaining his goal—for example, helping him to establish realistic expectations or arranging steps in his program that assure success—he must increasingly assume more responsibility for directing himself. Musical progress can, in the end, be made only through his own efforts; it cannot be achieved for him.

MUSIC PROVIDES FOR DEVELOPING OTHER-DIRECTED BEHAVIOR. In group settings, the individual must learn to subordinate his performance to that of the group. An awareness of the performance of others, and of his own in relation to theirs, is constantly required in the process of achieving appropriate musical expression and interpretation. Control of the self in relation to behavioral patterns of the group is necessary.

Music Enhances Verbal and Nonverbal Social Interaction and Communication

Most social occasions are accompanied by music, which generally increases sociability. With music in the background, many individuals find it easier to talk with others. In psychotherapy, patients often talk more freely in the presence of music. They may express in music or through musical preferences feelings not otherwise expressible. *Music may speak where words fail.*

Music Provides for Experiencing Cooperation and Competition in Socially Acceptable Forms

The very nature of music makes possible the experiencing of socially acceptable forms of cooperation and competition, singly or in combination. Musical groups not only require the individual to cooperate, but also offer him the opportunity to compete musically. Also, he may compete with himself, striving always to improve his performance; no degree of excellence of which he is capable and to which he might aspire is denied to him.

Music Provides Entertainment and Recreation Necessary to the General Therapeutic Environment

Diversional and recreational activities are a necessary part of institutional routine. Performances by community musical organizations, individuals, and stage groups can assist the patient in maintaining a general morale that may make specific therapeutic goals easier to attain. Such activities also permit him many experiences common to the world outside the institution. Although these activities are desirable, they should not be confused with formal music therapy procedures specifically designed with therapeutic intent.

Music Provides for Learning Realistic Social Skills and Personal Behavior Patterns Acceptable in Institutional and Community Peer Groups

Music skills usually enable individuals to interact more successfully in community groups. Dancing and other musical skills may help the patient participate with more poise and less need for defense. Musical groups in the community are becoming more available and usually require minimal financial and social prerequisites.

Some individuals possess asocial characteristics of which they are unaware. Others know very little about personal hygiene and acceptable modes of dress. Musical situations can be especially structured and in many cases provide the necessary motivation to bring about an improvement in these areas of behavior; such matters often greatly influence the individual's success or failure in his environment.

[Summary]

Music therapy uses the methods of a behavioral science and, as such, requires a theoretical formulation of its processes. To construct such a formulation has been the purpose of this chapter. The formulation is not proposed as a set of "true" laws and relationships. It is, rather, an attempt to integrate into one system the best knowledge and thought *presently available* concerning the function of music in therapy. Its orientation or integrating focus is the behavior of the individual when involved in a musical experience.

A theoretical formulation such as this may suffer one of several fates: It may pass into history having received little consideration. It may be examined and found wanting, but because of the study it required, result in a different, more adequate formulation of theory. Finally, it may prove of enough interest and worth to be put to the test in practice and research—to be modified, improved, and expanded. Hopefully, the latter fate will come to pass. In any case, processes in music therapy take place *by uniquely involving* the individual in experience within structure, experience in self-organization, and experience in relating to others.

Chapter Two

A Re-Vision and Expansion of Processes in Music Therapy

The teacher who walks in the shadow of the temple,
among his followers,
gives not of his wisdom but rather of his faith and his
lovingness.
If he is indeed wise he does not bid you enter the house of
his wisdom,
but rather leads you to the threshold of your own mind.
For the vision of one man lends not its wings to another
man.

Kahlil Gibran

Editor's Introduction

This is the first of two papers presented at the National Association for Music Therapy 30th annual conference, Dallas, TX, October 30–31, 1979. For some years prior to delivering the present address, Sears had ruminated over weaknesses in the original Processes. He had even challenged students to design models to better express them. When new ideas began to emerge in his head, he said they came from the unconscious as a "re-vision." This "re-vision" led him to a well-regarded theory of intelligence titled "Structure of Intellect" developed by the late psychologist J. P. Guilford, and opened the door to a new and different way of perceiving the Processes.

Origin and Purpose of Processes in Music Therapy

In 1964, twelve music therapists came together to codify the operating processes and principles in music therapy. The profession had been in existence for only twenty years or so, and a strong theoretical foundation had not yet been established. During the course of this symposium the group came up with all kinds of ideas by utilizing brainstorming techniques. One of the documents that resulted became Chapter 2 in *Music in Therapy*—"Processes in Music Therapy" (Sears, 1968).

At the time the book was written, music therapists were employed primarily in mental hospitals, and were just beginning to gain access to mental retardation facilities. That chapter tried to say that the music therapy process does not depend upon a particular philosophy or treatment concept within a given situation. Whether one would use the Processes as a gestalt technique, behavior modification technique, or whatever other technique one might choose, it seems that these things are in operation regardless of the so-called climate in which music is being used. There is something about music itself that is its own, and is not dependent upon being connected to a specific therapeutic technique or system. The Processes come pretty close to achieving that, but there are elements of Existentialism in their expression. For example, the word "experience" is used like the existentialists use "being," meaning the experience of the moment or of successive moments.

Over the years, as the Processes were evaluated and scrutinized, the need for a major revision emerged, both in the way they were presented and in some of the terminology. The essential ingredients, those being the three types of experiences labeled *classifications,* which in the text are defined as "broad concepts" or "categories" respecting the uses of music as therapy, were still central to the entire concept. However, they presented a confusing picture to some readers. To many people, it appeared as though there was a linear relationship. Indeed, the configuration *was* linear—it was flat. It did not show the interaction and interrelations among the three generic classifications of *structure*, *self-organization*, and *relating to others*. The notion of a three-dimensional activity was omitted. In addition, readers found duplication between the *self-organization* and *relating to others* classifications, although that may have been the result of inaccurate choices of words in the outline rather than any cognitive misunderstanding I had about the meaning of the classifications.

Originally, when the book was being prepared as part of a government grant, each person who wrote a case history was supposed to annotate back to the Processes chapter as to what seemed to be going on in that particular case history. Looking at the Processes linearly, they never really represented what the case history reported because the Processes as presented were one-dimensional, whereas in almost every statement in the case history, the three dimensions showed up in the same statement. So, if one tried to cover a statement with one item of the Processes, only a part of the statement in the history was being described. It became impossible to use the Processes as an evaluative tool. Thus, Chapter 2's main deficiency is that because of the effect linearity gives, it is impossible to cross-reference case history data with the Processes. This troubled me and demanded correction if the Processes were to continue to be useful.

Original Processes in Music Therapy and Time-ordered Behavior

The outline of the Processes which appeared in Chapter 2 of *Music in Therapy* (Sears, 1968) should not be substituted for the entire chapter because there is a lot of philosophy in the text which cannot be reduced to an outline. In fact, to understand the outline, one must read the accompanying text. For example, the musical experience itself assumes many different forms—listening, active participation, and so on.

Yet even the text, at least in one instance, is vague at best or misunderstood at the extreme, this being the section, "music demands time-ordered behavior," a component of the first classification, *experience within structure.* It is doubtful that the reader comprehended the full meaning of this pronouncement, tucked away, as it were, even though the first sentence declares that music's unique structure is its existence through time (Sears, 1968). It is the "art of time."[1]

However, notwithstanding individual exceptions, the process itself seems to have to work regardless of the character of the involvement. It is not dependent upon a specific physical setting—specific people, specific music, or any of the other attendant factors. It is a driving force unto itself.

Also, the chapter is limited to a discussion of the musical paradigm itself. Those aspects of music therapy that are common to most therapies are omitted to a large extent. This information is not found in the outline, but rather in the discussion. It must be emphasized that the three Processes classifications are not linear. This notion, which the chapter narrative fails to dispel, continues to confound the reader. There is no pure progression from lower to higher levels because a true rank order of the classifications does not exist.

There is always a constant mixture of experiences. When a client is working alone in a practice room he would be experiencing certain parts of *self-organization.* Assuming he is practicing music, which is the reason for him being there, he would be experiencing the *structure* of the music. But, he would not be relating to other people. Two of the three classifications would be in operation. However, within the usual therapeutic session there is a client, a therapist, and a structure. Thus, there would exist a mixture of

---

[1] J. T. Fraser (1999) understood this when theorizing about the origins of music. To simplify his erudite remarks, the "musical present"—which is the only reality in music we are able to experience, is synchronous with the organic and mental presents, e.g., the life process, the awareness of existence. When the "musical present", e.g., the composition or "piece," makes contact with the organic and mental present, i.e., the human being, the result creates "musical memories and anticipations and, with them, the musical experience of time's passage" (p. 138).

all three classifications. From these examples it is valid to assume that at any one time at least two of the three experiences are in operation.

Although a limited degree of order of progression does exist, the Processes are not classically hierarchical in structure or operation. Certainly, the *experiences within structure* are foundational in character for the other classifications. However, the constructs need not occur in the order presented in the outline nor before one begins to work on any of the constructs in the other two classifications. Nor, in all probability, will all of the constructs be achieved in the course of therapy. *Relating to others* implies some prior success in *self-organization*, but it is not necessary to achieve all of the *self-organization* constructs before being able to relate to others.

This chapter also fails to communicate clearly the most important concept of the three experiences, this being the concept of relationship. Specifically, there exists a music environment inhabited by therapist and client. From this environment a relationship develops between the two individuals which gradually expands to increasing numbers of people. It is incumbent upon the therapist to create the appropriate environment and shape the interaction so that a sound relationship can emerge. Upon this hinges successful therapy. That is quite a burden for one person. Music therapy is as much about relationships as about music.

The "Processes in Music Therapy" may have been misconstrued in other ways over the years because they are not accurately presented in the outline, nor does the source text clarify their meaning. As originally presented in E. Thayer Gaston and Erwin H. Schneider (1965), *An Analysis, Evaluation, and Selection of Clinical Uses of Music in Therapy*, the Processes were expressed in a taxonomic format. Table 1 is a merger of that with the outline. In this grant-supported work, the organizing system was explained as follows: "The whole number shows the broad classification; the tenth, the construct; and the hundredth [where it occurs], a sub-construct. The processes are then presented as behavioral definitions for each construct insofar as is possible" (p. 32).

Editor's Note: Some numerical values in Table 1 have been changed by the Editor. For example, in the original work, some tenth (construct) and one-hundredth (sub-construct) figures were expressed in odd rather than consecutive numbers. No explanation for original numbering has been found.

Unfortunately, in the Macmillan publication, this explanation, which is critical to the understanding of the system, was omitted and an outline replaced the taxonomy. These alterations resulted in the erroneous impression that each third level subsume (the hundredth) in the outline represented a *process* rather than a *sub-construct* as was the actual case. To correct this error, it must be understood that the process "describe[s] the manner in which the behavior of the individual is affected according to the construct [or sub-construct]" (Sears, 1965, p. 30). It is *not contained within the outline per se* but, instead, constitutes the discussion of the constructs which *follows* the outline. An example may serve to clarify. "Music provides a means for self-expression," a construct in the self-organization classification, discusses the role music plays in influencing certain behaviors such as choice, adaptability, transference, and decision-making, all which are aimed toward a more positive self-image. Of course, all discussion centers around behavior and experiencing.

At this point in the discussion, a review of the definition of terms used to describe the organizing system in the original Processes texts is in order. *Classification,* of which there are three, "signifies a general idea, a broad concept or category, concerning the use of music in therapy. . . . A *construct* [or sub-construct] attempts to propose formally, to define and to limit, an explicit relationship between music and the behavior of an individual" (Sears, 1968, p. 31). Specific constructs are identified as inherent within each of the three major classifications. *Process* is defined in the foregoing paragraph.

Table 1
Outline of the Processes in Music Therapy Classifications and Constructs

1.00 Experience within structure
    1.10 Music demands time-ordered behavior
        1.11 Music demands reality-ordered behavior
        1.12 Music demands immediately and continuously objectified behavior
    1.20 Music permits ability-ordered behavior
        1.21 Music permits ordering of behavior according to physical response levels
        1.22 Music permits ordering of behavior according to psychological response levels
    1.30 Music evokes affectively-oriented behavior
    1.40 Music provokes sensory-elaborated behavior
        1.41 Music demands increased sensory usage and discrimination*
        1.42 Music may elicit extramusical ideas and associations
2.00 Experience in self-organization
    2.10 Music provides a means for self-expression
    2.20 Music provides compensatory endeavors for the handicapped individual

2.30 Music provides opportunities for socially acceptable reward
and non-reward
2.40 Music provides means for the enhancement of pride in self
2.41 Music provides means for successful experiences
2.42 Music provides means for feeling needed by others
2.43 Music provides means for enhancement of esteem by
others
3.00 Experience in relating to others
3.10 Music provides means by which self-expression may be
socially acceptable
3.20 Music provides opportunity for individual choice of response
in groups
3.30 Music provides opportunities for acceptance of responsibility
to self and others
3.31 Music provides for developing self-directed behavior
3.32 Music provides for developing other-directed behavior
3.40 Music enhances verbal and nonverbal social interaction and
communication
3.50 Music provides means for experiencing cooperation and
competition in socially acceptable forms
3.60 Music provides entertainment and recreation necessary to the
general therapeutic environment
3.70 Music provides means for learning realistic social skills and
personal behavior patterns acceptable in institutional and
community peer groups

Adapted from Sears, 1968, pp. 33–34.

*Not included in *Analysis, Evaluation, and Selection of Clinical Uses of
Music in Therapy*. It was added later to *Music in Therapy*.

Processes in Music Therapy: Revised Model

The primary purpose for revising the Processes was to organize them into
an understandable and readily usable order. In fact, this is not a true
revision, but a progression from and a building upon the original.

It aims to permit the insertion of the particular therapist back into the
individual practice of music therapy—the "you" that only *you* can give. By
that is meant that so much of our practice has been modeled after that of
fine leaders, people who themselves have proven their therapeutic
excellence. However, much of what they present to us is *them*. They have
certain equipment, individualized charts, special techniques, and unique

styles. But that is not you nor me. Nor can a valid discipline rest upon such a system.

To conceive an appropriate system which would dispel the linearity misconception that the Processes presented did not come easily. Through all the struggle the answer had to come from the unconscious as a re-vision. I cannot consciously recall the thinking process that occurred. The stimulus which seemed to be most compatible with my purpose finally came from a three dimensional cube model—the Guilford Structure-of-Intellect model (1967).

Using the Structure-of-Intellect (SI) as a model, I organized the Processes into a circular configuration. That model is present in Figure 1. This configuration has a practical value, which I will explain later.

Organizing the Processes around verbal descriptors is a completely arbitrary system. The words themselves are not intended to be absolutes. They should not mean anything specific, but instead should be concepts to think *about* and to think *with*. Granted, the words do have meaning in the therapeutic sense, and it is expected that they will be useful to the therapists. However, they should serve primarily as springboards to launch one into ever widening exploration into the uses of music as therapy.

The "Processes in Music Therapy" model is structured around time-ordered behavior because that is fundamental to all of the factors inherent in the musical experience. Thus, *time-order* is spread across all levels of the Processes. To graphically show this, the model has been shaded. The shading represents time-ordered behavior. The small arrows placed arbitrarily at the edges of the circles in Figures 1–5 indicate that there is always interplay among the three classifications.

In the original Processes outline, "time-ordered behavior" is placed as a construct within *experience within structure*. If you ever perceived it in that restricted sense, forget it now. Of course, the text of that chapter states that it is fundamental to all the other constructs and describes it as the working principle of music. However, because an outline is often digested more easily than prose, many people accepted what they saw in the outline.

Taking the three classifications and considering any situation which incorporates experiencing, it is possible to make all kinds of connections with philosophy for thought. The Processes are a trinity of you, what you do and how you go about it, and your relation to others or the environment. That dictated the original use of the words *structure*, *self-organization*, and *relating to others*.

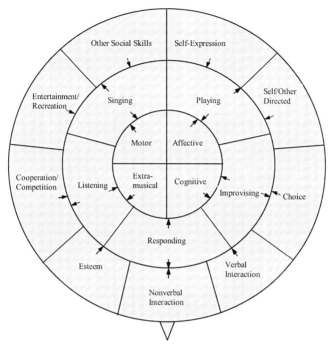

Structure: inner circle; Self-organization: middle circle; Social Relations: outer circle; ◯: time-ordered behavior

Figure 1. Processes in music therapy model. Adapted from Sears (1968).

The word "experience" is further used mainly to signify the one unique factor which exists in music, that being the beginning of a "now" moment, and always being required to go into the future in the time-ordered structure of the music. From there it required only a bit of logic to deduce that the time-ordered concept must be expanded to the total inclusiveness of the Processes. It is not a statement of process restricted to a single classification—structure. Any theory of music automatically presupposes time-order. We do not give it much thought while practicing, composing, or listening to a concert. Of course, music does not exist without it, nor do a myriad of other realities—the human body, for example. But, for music therapy purposes, we must commit to the concept that time-order at the very minimum is a theoretical posture. This is a major change in the Processes which aims to clarify meaning.

The word "time" means, for the most part, what we experience moving into the future. "Order" is how we chop time apart. I have come to learn that in some mystical societies it is believed that the universe was ordered and made solid, and space became because God, or whoever created the universe, vibrated time. From that beginning, our concepts of both time and space originated from the utterance of the first sound, whether it was "Let there be light," or some other pronouncement. It was sound that brought the universe into being.

The Processes model has been designed as three concentric circles. The inner circle denotes the musical *structure* of the therapeutic situation. There is something the therapist hopes is occurring inside the client, which is represented by the middle circle, *self-organization*. *Social relations,* which seems to be our therapy purpose, is the outer circle.

In the original Processes (Table 1) this third classification is identified as *relating to others*. All three classifications point to the center, which is the therapist,[2] who must decide how to manipulate the total arrangement to achieve the desired musical experience. Such physical structure decisions as whether or not the drapes are pulled, whether the air conditioner continues to run or not, how the furniture shall be arranged must be made. Then the therapist must decide what he/she wants to start happening and, in a sense, what features of these structures exist in the state the client is in. There are so many decisions to make.

Each circle in the diagram should not be joined nor would it ever be. That is, each circle should be drawn so that it is not closed, symbolizing that the whole system of music therapy is still wide open, awaiting further expansion and modification as new information about music and/or human behavior surfaces. Each circle can expand with additional thought possibilities. Nor are the circles fixed one to another. They are meant to be rotated, thereby allowing each construct within a given classification to be matched with another in each of the other two classifications.

Imagine, if you will, the model as a spiral—a double helical model much like the DNA graphic design. [The late] Marie-Louise von Franz (1978), world-recognized Jungian psychologist, suggests that the DNA design of living organisms is an apt analogy "to the archetypal ideal of time as a spiral, which reconciles the linear and cyclic aspects of time" (p. 19). J. T. Fraser labeled these "aspects of time" as "knowledge" (linear) and "passion" (cyclic) times, respectively (see "Time, the Servant of Music," "Fusion and Confusion," Chapter 6). David Epstein (1981) also subscribes

---

[2] Sears did not show the therapist in the model, possibly because the model as presented graphically is two-dimensional and thus does not readily lend itself to such a display. The Editor has experimented with several three-dimensional designs which place the therapist at the center of each classification. However, whether Sears would find these acceptable cannot be confirmed. In full accord with his philosophy, the reader is encouraged to design his or her own model to incorporate the missing therapist.

to an open circular musical world, actually more like von Franz's DNA model. Through interconnections we are carried into deeper levels of musical meaning. The key, he surmises, "lies in the structuring of time" (p. 197).

This configuration has a practical value as well. It visually shows the interactions and interrelations among the classifications, which was a deficiency of the original Processes. Specific descriptions of the classifications and their related human behaviors and operations here follow.

Description of Processes Classifications

Structure: human behaviors required by and inherent in musical experience
>   Motor: natural body responses to music; requires sensory input and includes rhythmic response
>   Affective: pleasant or unpleasant influences based in part on past experiences; physiological factors can contribute
>   Cognitive: process of intellectual learning; includes reflection which is a product of learning
>   Extramusical: stimuli which surround the music both in external environment and musical accoutrements; thoughts evoked within listener

Self-organization: inner responses; personal attitudes, interests, values, and appreciation which are impacted by the musical experience; concerns how one expects the client to operate
>   Responding: simplest form of behavior, is manifest in many ways, both observable and inferred
>   Listening: intentionally attending to music in a passive manner
>   Singing: active music-making requiring highly personal involvement and expression because production emanates from inner physical and emotional levels
>   Playing (instrumental): high level operation requiring knowledge of complex mechanics involved in producing musical sound
>   Improvising: ability to apply basic compositional (theory) rules to a composition to produce a new and different musical product based upon the original

Social Relations: behavior of individual within the musical experience in relation to other individuals, singly or in groups
>   Self-expression: ability to express feelings, both transitory and continuing, through music

Self/other directed: opportunity to accept responsibility in a musical environment as this relates to self and others; goal-setting is basic technique

Choice: opportunity for individual decision-making; freedom to choose can be as (more) important as (than) the choice

Interaction factors:

1. Nonverbal: music is a vehicle of communication when words are too threatening

2. Verbal: music in environment can enhance communication by shifting focus/subject from sensitive, uncomfortable areas which tend to shut down verbal interaction

Esteem: sharing or contributing to successful music experiences with others produces praise from others; sense of worth received from such praise

Cooperation/competition: ability to work with others to achieve a common goal; to compete with self and others to hone music skills is inherent in very nature of music

Entertainment/recreation: provides enjoyment either through participation or observation/listening; nature of music is to provide aesthetic experiences

Other social skills: ability to behave at a socially elevated level due to the structure inherent in (required by) musical situation; public performance requires specific mode of behavior and can teach self-confidence, dress, and hygienic etiquette

Discussion of Processes Classifications

Structure classification. This classification "refers to those behaviors of an individual that are required by and are inherent in musical experience" (Sears, 1968, p. 34). The construct labeled *motor* connotes sensory input and includes rhythmic response. Basically, however, it concerns our natural body responses to music that we learned as children before we were forced to cognize music.

Affective comes next because from the moment we learn anything, whether it is so-called cognitive or not, we seemingly start to develop an affective filter. The filter is determined by the addition of all of our pleasant and unpleasant experiences. The moment eventually arrives when we do not even allow certain notions into our head because they are so contrary to our prior conditioning that we have developed preconceived biases and thus block them from awareness. This is affective behavior plus emotional behavior. Physiological behavior and physiological measures are included in this construct.

The *cognitive* construct, which has been impressed upon us from the day we were born, is the process of intellectual learning. This construct also includes reflection, which is a product of cognition. Clients come to the music situation from a variety of cognitive levels based upon prior musical and nonmusical learning. This learning continues in any musical activity, not only in a structured music therapy or appreciation class.

Extramusical factors would include the environment, for example, the lighting, the furniture, the physical arrangement of the group, e.g., standing, sitting on chairs or floor. These factors are all of the stimuli that surround the music. Although they are generally associated with the environment, there are also cognitive processes that are extramusical, such as when one recognizes that blowing into a horn at one end will produce a sound from the other. That is not a musical factor. Rather, it is an acquired item of information of an extramusical nature, which we think is so obvious. We have been taught that this is part of the music, but it is not. Music is the sound. This construct has been broadened from the original Processes in which it pertained only to the thoughts that the music evoked within the individual.

Self-organization classification. This second level concerns how one expects the client to be operating. It is intended to verbally identify what the word "self-organization" means in a *musical* context. The original Processes avoided that, and instead presented only ideas about the affective operations. It stated that self-organization "is concerned with inner responses which may be inferred only from behavior, and has to do with a person's attitudes, interests, values, and appreciations, with 'his meaning to himself'" (Sears, 1965, p. 37). Through this omission (musical context), the distinction between this classification and *relating to others* was vague. For example, there is not much difference between the construct "music provides for self-expression," and the one in the *experience in relating to others* classification, "music provides for self-expression in a socially acceptable way." These were too closely associated in meaning, and thus people had trouble sorting them apart to see what the difference may be. By shifting terminology to specific operations in which the client is engaged in the process of becoming organized, e.g., listening, singing, improvising, it is hoped the confusion is eliminated. The rationale will be pressed further in the discussion of the Processes and another model, the Structure-of-Intellect, later in this chapter.

The factors that impact upon self-organization are the possible ways the music becomes operational: *responding, listening, singing, playing, improvising.* The client is expected to be engaged in a specific musical operation, the simplest being responding. Responding can be manifest in a variety of ways, although not all are directly observable. *Listening* is the next least complex factor. *Singing* and *instrumental playing* are distinctly different from one another. The singing voice is the more personal of the two, until, that is, we psychologically own our external instrument and it becomes part of our being. When we psychologically own our instrument, the sound we mentally want to produce emerges before we have time to think about it. Through practice we have forgotten the technical factors required to produce that pleasing sound. These technical factors have been internalized, and thus we become the music. It is another *time-order*.

Improvising is the most sophisticated operation and probably the least utilized in treatment. There is a reason, of course, because it requires creativity, flexibility, and some analytical ability, all which do not come easily for many clients. Yet, when one can dare to feel free enough to impose one's own musical ideas on established musical compositions, the inner being will probably be free to express the self.

The constructs in this classification are somewhat hierarchical although, as the arrows indicate, they do interact with the other classifications. By analogy, one cannot ask an intelligent question without having at least a feeling for the answer.

Social relations classification. At this third level, interaction among individuals is involved, and it is toward this interaction that the constructs are directed. This is the level of expressing self, taking self as a directive process, and taking directions from others. Two constructs in particular, *verbal* and *nonverbal*, have been specifically classified as interaction and communication constructs.

The constructs are hypothesized to fall into one of two categories: those that are (a) inherent within the music experience, that is, the dynamic effects of the experience, and (b) potential outcomes of the musical experience, that is, the residual effects the experience may have upon the individual. Although an argument can be made that all constructs will contain both attributes, it is feasible to conclude that the constructs constitute a broad spectrum of relating-type experiences, and thus could logically more frequently fall into one category or the other.

Therefore, based upon the premise that all constructs will fall primarily into only one category—although not be excluded from the other—an arrangement can be made as follows. Constructs which are primarily inherent within the musical experience are *nonverbal*, *cooperation/competition*, *entertainment/recreation*, and *choice*. Constructs which are primarily outcomes of the musical experience are *esteem*, *other social skills*, *self-expression*, *self/other- directed*, and *verbal*.

The primary criterion for assigning constructs was immediacy of response. Those constructs which were most apt to occur immediately were classified as inherent within the musical experience, while those which generally would require long-range development were considered as outcomes of the experience.

What this model seeks to show is that there is always something of the musical structure present, which is essentially what *structure* means. There is always something going on inside the patient—he is self-organizing himself. Finally, there is always some relationship, at least with the therapist.

The model resulted in a rather phenomenal number of thought processes, as will be explained later in the combined SI-Processes in Music Therapy models, (Figures 3–5). Suffice it to say that at this juncture, 180 different experiences are identified in the Processes. The constructs are multiplied further by the very fact that each individual can take any one of these words and produce many different instances of experiences, and therefore multiply the whole model again by the number of people who participate and all the separate ideas *they* have. It is a generative, not an explicit system.

Structure-of-Intellect Model

The next step in the revision process was to correlate the Processes model with Guilford's theory of intelligence, the Structure-of-Intellect (SI) model (1967) (see "Models for Thinking," Chapter 3, for original model [Figure 2] and complete discussion of SI). In order to more easily transfer concepts between the two models, I redesigned Guilford's model from its original three-dimensional cube shape into a circular arrangement. Figure 2 is that redesign.

Guilford organized his model into three categories of intellectual abilities: *contents, operations, and products. Contents* applies to the raw materials of information in the head (or the person), or what you want to put into that organism. It is at least a bi-directional operation. The raw information is then processed into major intellectual activities, or O*perations*. The forms that this information takes as the individual continues processing it is the *products* category. A combination of one item from each of the three categories constitutes an intellectual factor or ability. Table 2 explains the model in limited detail.

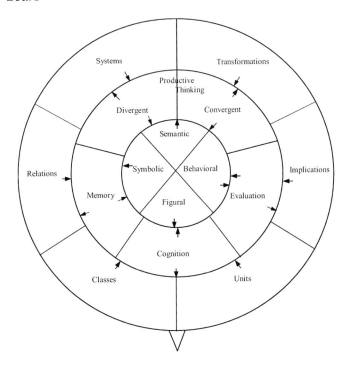

Contents: inner circle; Operations: middle circle; Products: outer circle

Figure 2. Structure-of-intellect model. Adapted from Guilford (1967, p. 63)

Table 2
Structure-of-Intellect

Contents	Kinds of information assumed existing or to be presented
Figural	Concrete information, the "thing" or phenomenon,
Symbolic	Arbitrary denotative signs, numbers, codes, letters, arrows, musical notations, etc.
Semantic	Word meanings and combinations
Behavioral	Primarily nonverbal information involved in interaction, including emotions, social intelligence
Operations	Individual's internal actions on contents
Cognition	Knowing, discovering, being aware of information; comprehending

Memory	Storing, retrieving information
Productive Thinking:	
Divergent	Generating new information from given information; emphasis is on number and variety of responses
Convergent	Generating unique, accepted solutions
Evaluation	Reaching decisions, judging appropriateness of information
Products	Results of operations on contents; the way information occurs
Units	Single, segregated items of information
Classes	Grouped information according to common properties
Relations	Connections between items and classes
Systems	Higher level connections into large organized wholes
Transformations	Changes in information usually from one form to another, music into painting, etc.
Implications	Predictions, extrapolations, or conclusions drawn from the information

Adapted from Guilford (1967).

The Combined SI–Processes in Music Therapy Models

Taking the three-dimensional concept from the SI model and applying it to the Processes brings forth some interesting comparisons. The Processes term *classification* can be perceived in the same context as Guilford's term *category*. Thus, the behaviors required and inherent in *experience within structure* bear similarity to what he identifies as *content*. *Experience in self-organization*, or organizing oneself, can be closely related by analogy to the *operations* one performs inside oneself. The *product* of music therapy is *experience in social relations*, and this seems to be an apt comparison also. By adopting the SI concept, the restrictions the linear attitude imposed upon the original Processes is eliminated.

From these two models, the music therapy Processes model produces 180 possible different combinations of experiences, and the SI model, 120 intellectual abilities. A combination is formed by a *structure*, a *self-organization*, and a *social relation* in the Processes model (4 structure constructs x 5 self-organizations x 9 social relations), or a *content*, an *operation*, and a *product* in the Guilford model (4 x 5 x 6 = 120).

The next step was to combine individual Processes classifications with their SI counterpart categories. The *structure-content* combination will produce sixteen thinking possibilities—four *structure* constructs times four *content* abilities (4 x 4 = 16). Figure 3 shows the result. The small arrows indicate that to make a combination you turn either circle so that a *structure* will line up opposite a *content*. For example, a specific musical selection which conjures up a specific event from one's past would be a figural-affective combination. Or, a musical selection which prompts one to get up and dance would be labeled figural-motor. The generative nature of the model is easily demonstrated when one considers the vast number of experiences that fall within either of these combinations. And there are fourteen more combinations in this classification alone!

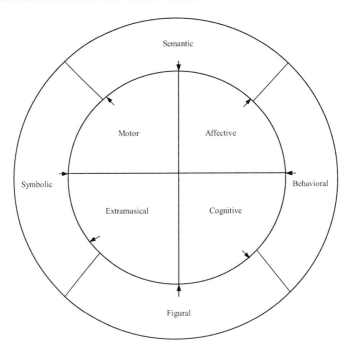

Experience within structure: inner circle; Contents: outer circle

Figure 3. Combined Sears experience within structure classification and Guilford contents category.

The five music therapy Processes of *self-organization* and the five from Guilford's *operations* category create *self-organizing operations*, as Figure 4 demonstrates, and produce 25 combinations of thought.

This classification (*self-organization*) of the original Processes seemed to be the weakest. The distinction between it and *relating to others* was not clearly made. However, when related to Guilford's *operations,* it gave me some insight into a different way of expressing the constructs. *Self-organization* is shaped by one's inner responses to external stimuli or experiences. Guilford's *operations* are the "individual's internal actions on contents," as stated in Table 2, or as Klausmeier (1966) puts it, "things that the organism does with the raw materials of information" (p. 35). What are the stimuli that create these inner responses upon which this classification is built? I did not consider this a factor in the original Processes, but comparing the constituents of the two categories indicated that the stimuli which shape *self-organization* are integral to this classification. Thus, the major change.

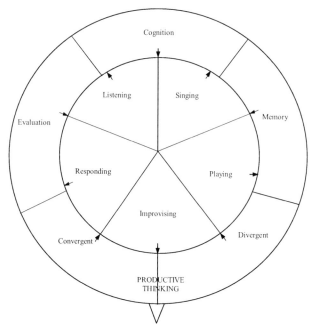

Experience in self-organization: inner circle; Operations: outer circle

Figure 4. Combined Sears experience in self-organization classification and Guilford operations category.

Improvising and *divergent thinking* have similar properties. They lead in a different direction from the information given, and what is most important, cannot be scored or rated as right or wrong. Guilford's factor is broader than the Processes construct, and would include composition, arranging, and tonal experimentation, to mention a few musical creative thinking activities. Thus, the two are not overlapping and do form a *bona fide* combination.

The final classification/category is *social relations* from the Processes and Guilford's *products,* as shown in Figure 5. Guilford (1967) defines *products* as the way information occurs. He also said the term "conception" is an apt synonym for "products." To carry this trend of thought a bit further, how should we define the word "information" in our model? Again I call upon Guilford. He states that "information," in the broadest term, is "that which an organism discriminates . . . within the psychological field, with no implication that the field is entirely conscious" (pp. 221, 249).

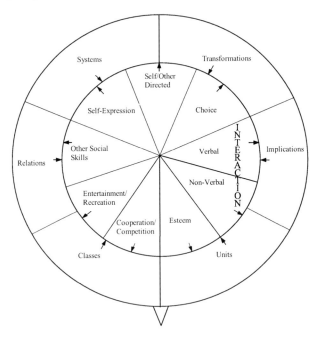

Experience in social relations: inner circle; Products: outer circle

Figure 5. Combined Sears experience in social relations classification and Guilford products category.

Relating all this to the Processes, the *product* of the music therapy experience is the ability to relate to others. Another way of thinking about this concept is that the product is the relationship per se. There is a difference in these two statements. Now, if we pick up on the word "discriminates," we can say that the factors in the *product* category—unit, classes, etc.—specify the various contexts within the musical experience at which social relations occur.

A *unit* is a "thing," that is, it is a discrete entity with distinct properties. It can exist without other products, whereas the opposite is not possible. Choosing a particular recording in a music listening session would be a possible units/choice combination.

An orchestra is an example of a *class*. It is a homogeneous group having a common purpose—to make music. Different instruments in that same ensemble have a relational factor to one another (violin + viola + cello + bass = string section). That same ensemble also could be classified as a system, particularly when in the act of musical production, although melody, harmony, and meter are more readily recognizable systems. Distinguishing between classes and systems is not always clear-cut, and Guilford's definitions are not that helpful when trying to decide if an orchestra is a *class* or a *system*. He states that *classes* are "recognized sets" while *systems* are "organized aggregates" (1967, pp. 80, 91).

At first glance, this category appears to be hierarchical, at least until we reach *transformations* and *implications*. However, except for *unit,* which must exist before the *products* category can operate, even the first four factors are not an absolute continuum. Relations between units can exist without regard for classes; systems do not presuppose relations; and so on. *Transformations* and *implications* are even less hierarchical in character. Yet even here a continuum can be perceived. The important argument against hierarchy in this category is that to make it so would restrict it to something unrecognizable by its creator. The nine *social relations* from the Processes with the six *products* from Guilford's SI model result in 54 combinations (9 x 6 = 54).

The combined SI-Processes models generate 21,600 specific thinking units or bits (16 x 25 x 54 = 21,600). That figure may sound astounding, particularly when one looks at these uncluttered and simplistic-appearing models. This is simply further evidence of the efficiency that is inherent in the models. Thinking with a model can allow for the amassing of more ideas and make it possible to keep them in mind more effectively for a longer period of time. How many more spoken words than have been set down to this point would be necessary to explain this concept without the benefit of these visual aids?

It is not necessary to memorize all of the individual items, although even that task is made easier through the efficiency of the model. Another advantage is that any new item of information can be added to the model with ease.

These individual thinking bits or combinations are not self-eliminating. All of the processes are operating concurrently, but the therapist's attention is concentrated upon a discrete selection in order to attain a specific treatment goal. Emphasis will shift from among the classifications/categories and between the combinations in each as the client's behavior changes. The interconnectedness of the total process is expressed in Figure 6.

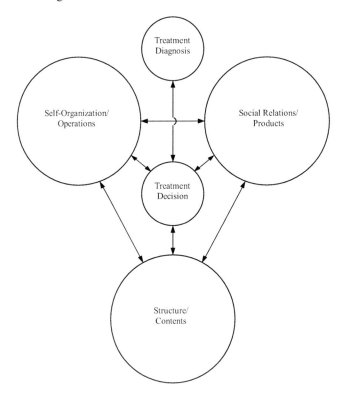

Flowchart showing interconnections among elements of music therapy process

Figure 6. Aids to Thinking.

Employing the model-building technique for music therapy would help us reduce the momentary aspect of our thinking to comprehensible dimensions. I selected Guilford's SI as a model for the Processes because I found it the most usable for me. However, one could insert almost any other model into the Processes which has a comprehensible number of parts, such as Gagné's conditions of learning (see "Models for Thinking," Chapter 3, Figure 1) or B. F. Skinner's operant conditioning. Other useful models to consider are those of Jean Piaget (human development), William J. J. Gordon (synectics creativity), E. Paul Torrance and Sidney J. Parnes (creativity), and Benjamin S. Bloom, David R. Krathwohl, and Anita J. Harrow (education).

Another shape this model can take is a technique called morphological analysis. To follow this technique, each classification/category item is written on a separate 3x5 index card, using a different color for each classification/category. The colored stacks are placed face down side by side and one card from each stack is turned up. Reading across the three, there will be one item each about *structure-content, self-organizing operations,* and *social relations products.* For example, one possible combination would be that "music provides a symbolically affective structure for evaluative listening in a system of self-expression." How beneficial this technique is will depend on the individual. However, it does expand our mental tool to incorporate some other kinds of concepts, and forces us to think in more expansive realms. This card-sorting technique does not require a computer. A colleague of mine went to the trouble to put it on computer. The resultant product was ridiculously thick—630 separate statements with all possible combinations of these 26 items. By contrast, one could take nothing more complicated than a set of 26 index cards, and play with them as long as one likes, and maybe come up with more and better ideas than what have been expressed here.

The Processes are not a fixed system. Indeed, flexibility is central to this revision, and without it its strength is diminished. Nor should the words serve any greater function than as stimulants to *your* thoughts. You are not supposed to think the way I did when I set them down. If it is confusing when I claim that there are 21,600 chances to think about music therapy, look at the model again. You will observe that at any one given time or within any one combination there are only six items to consider. Compare this with any page of music. Consider the number of notes on that page, the number of simultaneous tones which comprise each chord, the dynamic and metrical markings, and the nuances of the vocal and/or instrumental sound. Now that's complicated! Our stimulus of music is more complicated than are the Processes.

The model is intended to clarify the Processes so that they may be singled out and made personal to you, the therapist. It does not have to be applied as outlined or as used by other therapists. It is intended to lend itself to further expansion and modification by the user, while at the same time expressing a single, unified system for music therapy.

The revision of the Processes is an ongoing project, always awaiting further revision and improvisation. It is not finished today, and I hope it never will be. The Processes are intended to help us think about our stimulus, music, and make it so understandable to ourselves that two things can happen: (a) we can put music into any situation, and (b) we can individually put ourselves into the situation with our own individualized set of skills, talents, understandings, and personalities. The point is, that we must find ways of transmitting the excellence of many music therapists to a system for all therapists, rather than an exclusive tool available only to a few. Only then will we be able to provide all patients and clients with the best health care possible.

Throw the Processes away just as you throw away a musical scale when you are in the act of making music. That, not the act of memorizing a number of related concepts, should be your purpose for studying them. What confuses most of us is that we foolishly believe that if we can only accumulate a large body of facts we will acquire knowledge. But we finally come to the realization that the only fact which is certain is that facts do not beget knowledge. Eventually we must forget the fact, because so long as the fact is standing in front of us, we think of the fact and not the task at hand.

Barbara Brown (1980) stated this very well in "the Brownenberg Principle," a term she coined that is a play on words and modeled after the Heisenberg principle of indeterminacy. The Brownenberg Principle states:

> If you are busy processing information in your brain, you can't know you are processing the information because the information being processed is occupying the same neuronal space that is needed to become aware of what is being processed.
>
> And of course, conversely, if you are aware of information that *has been* processed, you can't be processing new information at that moment of awareness because the mechanisms for awareness occupy the same neuronal space needed to process the new information. (p. 263)

That is, we human beings have no conscious awareness of the nature of our own mental processes. It therefore follows that the body performing the music cannot perform it while engaged in the process of thinking about performing it.

This is patterned after the Heisenberg indeterminacy or uncertainty principle in quantum physics, which shows that, simply stated, an electron cannot look at another electron. Heisenberg's uncertainty principle shook the very foundations of the scientific community, for he proved that at the subatomic level exact science does not exist. Instead, only probabilities apply. It is upon this principle that the non-deterministic character of quantum physics rests. "These limits are not imposed by the clumsy nature of our measuring devices or the extremely small size of the entities that we attempt to measure, but rather by the very way that nature presents itself to us" (Zukav, 1979, pp. 132–133)—in a sense, hazy and ill-defined.

The whole of human science has this particular problem because humans are trying to look at other humans. The time scales on which we move, move together. Results in the basic sciences occur when the everlastingness of something outlasts us or is smaller than us. The farther these time distances are between the two relative scales, the better we can control the scientific product.

The Heisenberg principle can be illustrated by the operation of the electron microscope. In the electron microscope electrons are generated by an interaction between a wire filament and a metal plate (or anode) close by. The positive charge of the anode attracts the negatively charged electrons from the filament. All of this occurs in a vacuum.

In the anode is a pencil-size hole through which the beam of electrons flow. These, in turn, are focused by a set of lenses onto a specimen. The electrons flow through the specimen, and the resulting pattern is projected onto a fluorescent screen. Interactions occur in this entire process, and certainly, modifications occur in the electron beam *and* in the specimen observed by the observer.

Nobody has seen an electron yet, but the effects on the thesis have worked out. They weigh the same in theory. They tend to have the same speed. However—and this is the essence of the uncertainty principle—it is not possible to determine both the position and speed of an electron at the same time. By observing its position, its speed is changed; and conversely, the more accurately its speed is determined, the more imprecise its position becomes.

Presumably, one of the strengths of the human being is that it has the ability to know that it is the organism that is doing the knowing. This is known as self-reflexivity, and so far as we know, only humankind among the four levels of being that have been identified thus far on our planet possesses this quality or power. Self-reflexivity is an awesome ability, and bears heavily on much of the matter in this work. It is also referred to in other chapters in different but related contexts. To the music therapist, Brown's law and the Heisenberg uncertainty principle can be simply transformed to mean that every time you exchange glances with a client or touch one another, both of you have moved from where you were. In music, the participants are moved along the same time line. The experience of oneness among many which results can be experienced in no other way.

Music is such a powerful tool! An eminent psychologist once remarked that when a music therapist is at a loss for words in the therapy situation, he is saved because he can go back to the music. The music is the message! It should be learnable no matter from which direction one comes. The importance, to me, is *you* the therapist first, *your* music second, and *your* ability to put the two together so that when the therapeutic or teaching situation is completed, you have forgotten what you did. Then, and only then, will you have communicated.

Editor's Summary

Like so many undertakings which metamorphose over time, Sears continually mined the "Processes in Music Therapy" more deeply, and eventually devised a revision, the present work. He created a more in-depth approach to the three classifications: structure, self-organization, social relations, around which the Processes are organized. But even if that had not been necessary, the textual format mistakenly presented the appearance of linearity, which is not the case, and which is corrected here.

Much more significantly, "music as time-ordered behavior" originally was literally embedded in the classification "Experience Within Structure." In point of fact, time actually exists throughout all of the classifications. It is the core of music and is in evidence under all musical circumstances. "Time is both the essential component of musical meanings and the vehicle by which music makes its deepest contact with the human spirit" (1988, p. 2). So says Jonathan Kramer, author, composer, and music professor at Columbia University. To not raise time to the pinnacle of music making and show it throughout all aspects of the Processes would have rendered a revision of the Processes meaningless.

Elevating "time-ordered behavior" was not the only change necessary to expand the meaning of the Processes and, paraphrasing Sears, to insert the particular therapist back into the practice of music therapy. A graphic model designed as three concentric circles was deemed the best vehicle for expressing the Processes. However, it was the Structure-of-Intellect model developed by the late psychology professor J. P. Guilford that gave Sears the seeds for a revision, and allowed it to take off to a higher and more meaningful level. The merger of the two models, herein expressed visually, produced a system that significantly expanded the music therapy processes to incorporate not only situational experiences (e.g., affective behavior, listening, self-expression) but also Guilford's intellectual abilities (e.g., semantic, classes, memory). The modified classifications/categories became "Experience Within Structure/Contents," "Self-Organization/Operations," and "Social Relations/Products." The combined system can generate an astounding 21,600 specific thinking units or bits which an individual is capable of producing. Although other models may be merged with the Processes, Guilford's SI model is so graphically explicit and comprehensive that it renders Sears' work more meaningful and inclusive of the actual clinical music therapy situation.

Sears speculated on the possibility for further revisions in the future, surmising that such depends upon the validity of this one and how well it is received. If it generates the creative juices in some readers, and we recognize that our thinking machine is continually evolving, other more sophisticated renderings could emerge one day.

References

Brown, B. B. (1980). *Supermind.* New York: Harper and Row.

Epstein, D. (1981). On musical continuity. In J. T. Fraser (Ed.), *The study of time, IV.* New York: Springer-Verlag.

Fraser, J. T. (1999). *Time, conflict, and human values.* Urbana: University of Illinois Press.

Gaston, E. T. & Schneider, E. H. (Eds.). (1965). *An analysis, evaluation, and selection of clinical uses of music in therapy.* (Cooperative Research Project No. F–044). Lawrence, KS: The University of Kansas.

Guilford, J. P. (1967). *The nature of intelligence.* New York: McGraw-Hill.

Klausmeier, H. J., & Goodwin, W. (1966). *Learning and human abilities.* New York: Harper and Row.

Kramer, J. D. (1988). *The time of music: New meanings, new temporalities, new listening strategies.* New York: Schirmer Books.

Sears, W. W. (1965). Processes in music therapy. In E. T. Gaston & E. H. Schneider (Eds.), *An analysis, evaluation, and selection of clinical uses of music in therapy.* (Cooperative Research Project No. F-044). Lawrence, KS: The University of Kansas.

Sears, W. W. (1968). Processes in music therapy. In E. T. Gaston (Ed.), *Music in therapy* (pp. 30–44). New York: Macmillan.

von Franz, M.-L. (1978). *Time: Rhythm and repose.* London: Thames and Hudson.

Zukav, G. (1979). *The dancing Wu Li masters.* New York: William Morrow.

Chapter Three

Models for Thinking

A map is not the territory it represents, but, if correct,
it has a similar structure to the territory,
which accounts for its usefulness.

Alfred Korzybski

Editor's Introduction

This chapter is a compilation of two papers on the topic of models. "Alternative Models in Music Therapy" was presented at the National Association for Music Therapy 26th annual conference, Kansas City, Missouri, November 20, 1975; and, "Model Building: A Tool in Music Teacher Education" was presented at the combined North Central and Southwestern divisional conference of the Music Educators National Conference, Omaha, Nebraska, April 4, 1975. The decision to consolidate these original presentations was based upon the significant amount of duplication that existed between them, and the appropriateness of the topic to music therapists and music educators alike.

Purpose and Value of Models

In approaching this topic, I found myself acutely aware of the role models in general play throughout our entire lives. One might legitimately hypothesize that physical and emotional growth and development of individuals and societies can occur only within an environment filled with models. Models drive the whole of our technological society. One need not leave the walls of one's house to understand that models first had to be constructed before actual building could commence. Acquiring the skills necessary to execute an athletic sport—even learning to walk—demand models, although we may not be conscious of their existence. Imagine trying to verbally instruct a one-year-old about the muscular mechanics required to take that first step. Music history and literature are often—actually, usually—taught by presenting models, that is, examples of form, style, instrumentation, social and cultural periods, and the like. One limited example to illustrate my case is the symphony from Haydn to Beethoven as a model of musical form. Of course, in the therapeutic milieu, we set up basic models. The purpose of a model is to economically show relationships, something words fail to achieve.

Yet there are other models, or their absence, which propel our lives. These are thinking or mental models. Thinking models "attempt to put order and system in what we do when we plan an interview, prepare a speech, . . . or attempt to stimulate our ability to think creatively" (Bois, 1966, p. 145). Lest the reader think that this statement made by J. Samuel Bois concerns only models constructed in one's head, its application to graphic models is just as credible. Whatever the structure, the goal of a model is to present a tight structure which organizes many parts into a compressed, cohesive whole.

A few years back, I directed a symposium which sought to lay the groundwork for developing a theory of music therapy. To help generate the creative juices, I distributed an array of standard models and explained how these could help in carrying out the task of the group present. Later in the two-day event, participants were asked to design their own models and share them with one another. One participant stated that she felt figural models were meaningful only after one had worked with them. She had difficulty following the graphic design of another participant and requested repeated explanations before she was able to internalize the concept behind the model. Simply looking at the graphs first without explanation rendered them meaningless. It was necessary that she personally engage in the exercise with the designer.

This appears logical until we encounter the extreme of this concept, for example, that every author should have experienced everything that he writes about. Some of the finest authors have never left their living rooms, so to speak. Should every composition teacher have created a musical composition? I think of Nadia Boulanger, who has not stirred the world with her compositions, yet she is the 20th century's most acclaimed composition coach. While we must have some prior understanding of the process of concept formation in order to engage in an activity as complex as model-building, this is useful only in allowing us to free ourselves vicariously in order to design a more simplified and meaningful communicative form, such as a diagram on a piece of paper, a story, or a musical composition. Then we can participate. We get caught in the chickens-and-eggs dilemma again. Ralph M. Stogdill, at a highly informative symposium on model-building a number of years ago, proclaimed that "a study in the process of model-building can be regarded as a study in the intellectual activities of the model-builder" (1972, p. 5).

Psychologically, modeling seems to force us to put back together in a visual or auditory sound structure the things we tear apart with words. If I want you to understand me, you must read a long series of verbal symbols put out one after the other in time. With words I am trying to draw a picture in the mind of the reader similar to the one that is in my head. This is well illustrated in the classroom when students are asked questions and their response is, "I know, but I just can't say." Part of their inability to construct verbal answers is that they have not yet tied the words to the images they have in their heads. They often do have the knowledge, but simply are unable to put it into verbally comprehensible terms.

The strength of the Einstein theory of relativity, ($E = mc^2$), is that it becomes a model from which many different kinds of pictures and subdivisions can be made. It expresses, so far as we know, the total idea of the composite energy in the universe as it is now. In four little symbols almost everything in life in a certain connection is expressed.

We need modeling, not because it looks good on paper and is fun to play with, but for efficiency and convenience. Visually, through a model we can make things static in time, thus enabling us to keep our position somewhat constant until there is need to expand again. With a model, one can see more aspects of a concept simultaneously than is possible with words. Often, after reading even a short paragraph one is unable to recall the theme, which was stated in the first sentence. In order to retrieve that theme it is necessary to go back and read that introductory sentence once again. With a picture—a model—a higher degree of retention is possible. The brain receives the picture and quickly transforms it into intellectual meaning.

Models are also more convenient and in some situations the only way to present a proposition. Testing a new automotive engineering design on a drawing board before going into production is obviously the only sound way to build an automobile. When seeking to determine the effects of an earthquake measuring 7.3 on the Richter scale in an urban area, model-building makes it unnecessary to wait until after the catastrophe occurs and then search through the rubble for answers.

> Models are supposed to represent phenomena (or sets of phenomena) and to show how the relevant theory is to be applied. It is not asserted that the model *describes* the phenomena, or more generally, that it describes reality; rather it is asserted that the phenomenon—or reality—behaves *as if* the model were descriptive. That is, the model functions as a metaphor. (Reese, 1971, p. 19)

These words of Hayne Reese are but another way of saying "A map is not the territory," but it is useful.

I must accent the importance of designing one's own models and finding applications for them instead of exclusively using the models designed by others. But first, one must gain experience in model building. I would not be so bold as to attempt to pass off the present discourse as a technical how-to-build-a-model exercise. The process is much too complex, and there are greater authorities than I to whom the reader can turn. Instead,

I will focus on several basic principles to keep in mind whenever one is in the company of models. First, one must practice by (a) selecting a body of discrete information and shaping it into a model, or (b) selecting existing models and applying them in different ways.

When building models, a necessary criterion is that the product must be testable at all its crucial points. A valid model displays its value, according to Guilford (1967), "in the testable problems that it generates and in the reasonable implications that flow from it for technological practices" (p. 48).

The Confusion of Words

It is strange what we do with words. The definitions change, not only over long periods of time, but also among different subcultures within the same time period. We previously labeled primitive cultures as being merely backward, then underdeveloped, then developing, and now they are the Third World. They are the same people with the same problems, in a sense, but we soothe our own conscience by changing the words to seemingly less offensive ones. The truth is hidden behind euphemisms.

This is a problem in music education also, and in all of education as well. We have changed the terminology we use from "music" to "elements," from "elements of music" to "music fundamentals," and now we call them "basic concepts." The trouble is, our words do not even make sense when we do that. For example, melody is not a concept; "melodiousness" is. We should not speak of music education any longer. We should speak of music*s* education. Linguists are not expected to know every language to be respected for their expertise. Yet we believe that all bona fide musicians should know everything about all kinds of music, especially the kinds that appeal to our specific interests.

Words like "idiot" have now been replaced by "handicapped," but who is handicapped, the idiot or us? It is a good question to consider to bring us back to reality. "Insane" has been substituted with "mentally ill," "emotionally disturbed," or simply "troubled," those terms being more respectable now. We change our labels because we are beginning to realize that the labels themselves fix our thinking into modes or models of thought which determine much of our behavior as therapists. When we rely on labels, we are always in danger of falling into the notion that it is the system that makes it work and not ourselves. We should be in control of the system rather than the system being in control of us. Wendell Johnson (1965) put it very well by saying, "in these worlds of words inside our heads, we hold ourselves captive" (p. 71).

Take the index finger, for example, when pointed upward. We know what it is. It is index finger. It signifies number one; at its command it brings a taxi to the curb; pressed to the lips it signals silence, or whatever else we have decided it will communicate. We give these figural gestures labels, and in so doing need not contemplate them any longer. They no longer live. The moment we open our mouths and speak, we leave reality. By implication, if I am hoping to say something meaningful with words, it must be recognized that the communication involved is an abstraction rather than the real thing. The real thing is one step abstracted when it is assigned a name.

The danger of living primarily in the world of language is that our world becomes static. We substitute abstraction for actual living. The confusion becomes even more pervasive when we put words onto paper. The printing press has contributed as much to vague and obscure thinking as to the spread of literacy by setting words into concrete, so to speak. By fixing words on paper their meanings have become frozen. They are dead. Words were made to *manipulate* stimuli in the world of reality, never to *be* that reality. Words kill. *You,* the individual, must give them life again.

This distortion is built into our lingual thinking habits. The English language is useful for scientific pursuits because it incorporates a two-valued system constructed on a subject-predicate syntax. However, because of minimal ranges or degrees of meaning and its weakness in relational concepts, our language sometimes causes us to think in peculiar and erroneous ways. The Chinese had to develop a new kind of structure built on the analytic style language in order to help close the gap in their deficiency in the sciences. Most Oriental languages are picture, that is, ideographic or composite, languages. Unlike Indo-European languages— that includes English—which are two-valued, Oriental languages are multi-valued. They cannot point to something specific and declare what it is, but instead, see most situations in varying shades of gray. The Navajo language has three numbers only—one, two, and many.

Since much of human learning occurs in a verbal environment, language determines, by and large, not only what we think, but how we think. One's mother tongue shapes thought itself, and in so doing influences one's culture. Our view of the world comes as much from the words inside our heads as from observations and experiences outside. My worldview is determined in a specific way because my native language is English. The Navajo embraces a different view because of his language. Within the context of language itself there are many different ways of molding one's thoughts, and one of the possibilities is playing with words.

Puzzle Game

I have used the puzzle *Hexed* (Kohner Brothers, 1972) to teach the concept of models, to demonstrate a number of different behaviors we humans exhibit, and to discover how amazing it is, with all of the potentialities in each of us, that we human beings get along so well together. *Hexed* is a puzzle game consisting of twelve pieces of plastic, each having a different geometric shape, which fit into a rectangular box. The purpose, of course, is to put the pieces back in the box. It sounds simple enough until one tackles the job.

Let us assume that *Hexed* is a symbolic representation, or a model, of a very restricted learning universe, much the same as we are born into. However, in this simplified universe we have only twelve things to learn. In the puzzle there are three green pieces, three red pieces, and the remainder of this particular universe is colored yellow.

What I normally do is show the class the completed puzzle and then throw the pieces out on the table and have the students as a group put it together. When all twelve pieces have been successfully returned to the box, we discover that the individual pieces are now in different locations than before. This universe is now painted differently. The two worlds do not resemble each other except that their geometric parts are identical. They are not fitted in the box the same way as before, but it is the same world, in a sense, because it is made up of the same twelve ingredients.

Observing the behavior of students as they work the puzzle is very interesting and insightful into the process of learning. I have identified five different types of players that emerge in the course of the play—the miser, the leader/non-leader, the "must fit," the "throw it away," and the inflexible.

The twelve pieces are spread on the table and everyone is eager to participate. The miser immediately picks up a piece to put in the box. If he cannot find a place for it at that moment, he will transfer it to his free hand. He grabs another piece and tries to place it, but if that one does not fit either, he repeats the same procedure as before. Very quickly, the miser has all of the pieces in his hand and nobody else is able to play.

Often, all except the last piece will fit, but that final piece needed to complete this universe is the same shape as one of the pieces that has already been used. All that remains is a piece—or notion, or concept, or viewpoint—that just will not fit. Some students will throw the piece away, thus the label "throw it away." This is essentially what some of us try to do with our lives. We meet something that does not fit, so we attempt to throw it away. That is another solution to the difficulty, but that course eventually leads to distortion, confusion, and a dead end—thus, an incomplete universe.

Other students, the "must fits," will try to force the piece into the wrong space or will go so far as to inquire if they may break the piece apart and put the broken bits in the vacant space. Because each piece is composed of five small squares arranged in different geometric shapes, that would be a solution. How does that compare with our behavior when we have to approach a new concept that just does not fit with what our established patterns or expectations are?

The inflexible player operates much like the "must fit" when the realization occurs that the present course he is pursuing will not result in successfully completing the puzzle. Rather than go back and change our minds, get reoriented to a different course, which in this puzzle requires that only one or perhaps two pieces be moved to produce a right solution, we insist that the world we have up to now is the very right world. We throw away, try to break, or rigidly refuse to move anything that does not fit.

Leaders and followers emerge as play progresses in the same fashion as can be observed in other group situations. At times an individual will aggressively take the lead at the outset, only to be replaced when the followers perceive him to be a "false prophet." When this occurs, a successor is not so easily proclaimed because the followers show greater restraint in pledging their allegiance a second time. Play will often be aimless and unproductive during this period. Thus, in the leader/non-leader model, game-playing emulates the larger society in yet another way.

There is the individual who, instead of remaining within the accepted two-dimensional model, creates a three-dimensional design by overlapping some of the pieces—the same puzzle, the same shaped pieces, but fitted together to create an entirely different look. Remember, this puzzle represents a limited universe, and as it presently exists. In our larger universe we observe similar behavior in creative individuals, revolutionaries, and visionaries—persons who either by predilection or compulsion see their universes in a very different way from the model that is laid before them.

Puzzle players exhibit varying degrees of anxiety during the course of play. For some, anxiety is primarily due to the competition existing within the group situation, and would not be evidenced while playing alone. However, the most frequently observed symptoms of anxiety stem from the puzzle itself. It is difficult for most persons to accept the high level of the challenge. After all, there are only twelve pieces, whose shapes are not unusual. Why doesn't the solution come more easily? How can such a simple looking puzzle be so maddeningly complicated? In the real life situation, we often experience the same dilemma. As therapists, we must help our patients deal with the anxiety they feel. We, the observers, oftentimes judge the anxiety to be excessive to the cause. If you have made such judgments about the patients encountered in your work, I suggest that playing *Hexed* will give you some additional insight.

In addition to the usual sensory perception problems, which educational psychologists for years have used puzzles to expose, *Hexed* players reveal varying capacities to envision the gestalt when the pieces are scattered on the table. Some players will repeatedly attempt to join pieces which cannot fit together. They will not take the time to think through the logic of their actions by visually checking the shape of the space against the available pieces. How often do we carelessly fail to use our sensory abilities, and even more frequently our mental abilities, in problem-solving situations?

Edward de Bono, in his book *Lateral Thinking* (1970), discusses this concept as it applies to the way the mind works. Sequence of play is not the key to a solution. It makes little difference which piece is *first* selected or where it is placed. Making the best use of information at each stage of play, which is known as the self-maximizing method, does not necessarily guarantee success. There comes a time when the pieces will not fit. "For this reason," de Bono explains, "the *arrangement of information is always less than the best possible arrangement,* for the best possible arrangement would be quite independent of the sequence of arrival of the pieces of information" (p. 35). That being the case, how can puzzle-solving ever be anything more than by chance? It is through insight that one is able to move toward maximum use of information and away from chance solutions. The order of "thinking" sets the outcome.

Another de Bono theory (1970) I find helpful is that when one reaches an obstacle to a solution, rather than giving up and backing off, one should just bounce off and go around the corner from the other side. It may not necessarily solve the puzzle, but you might find a better problem hiding behind the one you set out to solve. For example, he offers a suggestion for dealing with pollution. If a company was required to put its intake water supply downstream from where the outflow is located, it would begin to voluntarily clean up its pollution.

There are over 2,339 ways to put these twelve pieces back in the box. When we look at our individual selves and consider how many "pieces" constitute our makeup—how many ways we can be shaped, we are shaped, or we shape ourselves—it is truly remarkable that we function individually and collectively as well as we do. If there are, in a sense, 2,339 ways to assemble twelve parts of a simple universe such as the puzzle *Hexed*, what are the dimensions of a given human being?

We continually try to recruit believers in our system. We tend to perpetuate that system because we rarely have asked any questions of our ancestors, even though we do not seem to like what went on in previous ages. This is what makes progress so slow. This is what makes changing constitutions, laws, and organizational structures lengthy processes if done democratically. A number of different kinds of opposing forces that inhibit change could be shown to be in effect.

One of these days someone may design a four-dimensional model of *Hexed*. The possibilities of the human mind and its constructs are unlimited. We do not know today what might be known tomorrow. Behavior modification may work today only because we have, in a sense, been taught that it works. B. F. Skinner himself has made the comment that we had better be aware that it is working, and that it is being used against us. Then we may be better able to defend ourselves and become something better than always being modified by somebody else's behavior.

Original Music Compositions

We do other unusual things in my classes to understand the concept of modeling. We build models upon musical compositions. Composers sought inspiration for their works in a variety of ways. Brahms, for example, used to walk through the woods listening to the sounds of nature. Then he went home and wrote a symphony! We might say that Brahms' system was to walk through the woods and listen to the birds—and that system produced great music! All composers, artists, and writers develop their individual models which stimulate the creative juices into action.

For this project, the class was divided into small groups, a teaching technique that I find successful. Each group was assigned to come up with its own extraction or abstraction from the environment in any way it cared to as the framework for an original composition. A minimal set of rules was given. These bore little resemblance to the highly structured rules of harmony music students are expected to learn in theory class. Music is one of the few fields in which the study of the theory of the field goes backwards in time rather than forward. At least, that is how it is brought to us when we are taught about it. Theory in mathematics, for example, looks into the future. The history is studied primarily as a springboard to propel one into the future.

The instructions for the class music compositions were simply to derive some system, make a translation into a musical sound—or what the group wanted to consider as musical sound—and orchestrate it for the group based upon the group's individual instrumental and/or vocal abilities. Each group performed its composition in "recital" for the other class members. A further requirement was to explain the model to the rest of the class so that everybody could understand the process employed to make the translation from the original model to the model of sound. The resultant products were not intended to be complete, ideal compositions. The purpose of the exercise was to demonstrate that if you realize that you can build a model and generate perhaps one new sound, and that if this exercise is performed three or four times you will have put together three or four new sounds, and that in the process you will have expanded self-awareness of the numerous possibilities for combining sounds.

Several of the compositions warrant description. A member of one group happened to be seriously interested in palmistry. The group decided to read the lines of one another's hands. They notated what each reading meant according to palmistry analysis, then performed a translation into musical notation, and produced a choral product.

In the second example, an instrumental ensemble, each person "played" what his or her polygraph line "sounded" like to him or her. Following a basic research design, the group administered polygraph tests to one another for a predetermined length of time. A brief aural stimulus was introduced during the testing period. The composition was written from polygraph readings.

This is not too different from the bio-music hypothesized by Barbara Brown (1974), respected biofeedback and mind authority. In her laboratory, primitive forms of bio-music were developed by transforming the body's biological signals into music—not simply sound, but aesthetically acceptable and recognizable music.

She sees bio-music as a futuristic form of therapy. For example, the music produced would be related to the subject's mood and sensations. The therapist would then analyze the physiologic activity which produced the composition. To capture or release a particular mood, the subject would attempt to duplicate those feeling states through the biofeedback process. Dr. Brown's bio-music is a rather heady concept, but one music therapists can understand and should explore.

The stimulus for the third example was human laughter. The group randomly recorded laughter, and selected the samples they wanted to imitate on their instruments. Each laugh was set into alternating A-B-A musical form, and was matched with the musical instrument to which it bore the closest characteristics of timbre.

A picture of a flower provided the centerpiece for yet another group. The piece was scored for trombone, flute, clarinet, and piano, those being the major instruments of the members. Each person selected a part of the flower, such as stem, petal, or leaf, and followed that line, playing what that part of the flower "sounded like" to him or her.

Another group, consisting of all vocalists, used the smooth and harsh vowel sounds in vocal exercises. The organizing principle was alternating smooth and harsh-sounding themes, which were expanded into a five "movement" work—smooth, harsh, smooth, harsh, smooth. Examples of other models were the system of mathematics, a gin rummy game, a boxing match, a women's lib argument, and chapters from Lundin's *An Objective Psychology of Music* (1967).

Again, it was not the intent of the exercise to teach composition, but rather to demonstrate that models are all around us and that we are constantly required to pick and choose from among them. It provides a means of generating ideas out of the environment from anything and everything. It provides the opportunity to stretch the imagination and search out relationships from among seemingly unrelated ideas.

Models also can be quite individualistic. That certainly is the case in the building process. Someone else's model may not be appropriate for you. As therapists, we meet people as individuals, whether it be in a one-to-one or group situation. In so doing, we need our own separate and distinct models.

I play the tuba and twirl baton, instruments which themselves are not considered standard in the traditional sense, yet they aptly demonstrate the notion that models can be found anywhere. Models are what we work with in our heads. There are all kinds of them, from simple one-step instructions to large general concepts. What are your models? You have the right and the need for a model.

The music therapy discipline has yet to discover its model. Oh yes, there are models, such as behavior modification *with* music, Gestalt therapy *with* music, auto-suggestion systems *with* music, developmental therapy *with* music. We concentrate more on the models that utilize music as a support for other therapies than on genuine music therapy models. All too often we perceive our discipline as an add-on rather than self-sustaining. I believe that our particular medium has something greater to offer, which has been so obvious that we have not even asked the right questions or looked for the right answers.

Learning theorists are inveterate model-builders, which is due in no small measure to the nature of their subject. I have chosen a few examples that I believe best demonstrate the validity of model-building as an aid to the therapy process. These are not to be memorized as models *per se*, but are cognitive devices to assist one to think about things.

Gagné's Types of Human Learning

This first example (see Figure 1) is built on the theories of [the late] Robert M. Gagné, the learning theorist who sought to integrate the total fields of all learning theories. My purpose in presenting it is that in my judgment the whole figure represents a model. Additionally, each of the six learning levels is a model also, thus we have models within a model. The diagrams called *paradigms*—yet another sub-model—sum up in a tidy notation system a complex idea of the entire range of learning as Gagné perceived it.

The model does not mean for me the so-called psychoanalytical, psychological, or emotional types of connotations we carry with us into our treatment concepts. Rather, it is a sequential, hierarchical patterning of the types of human learning. Much of what we do in music therapy, in my estimation, is at that first level, *response learning*. We work with total bodily response—stimulus-response ideas.

Later, Gagné (1965) refined his ideas about learning and divided *response learning* into two types—*signal learning* and *stimulus-response learning*. *Signal learning* is the classical conditioned response discovered by Pavlov in his experiments with dogs. This learning involves a real connection between stimulus and a natural or "involuntary" response. It usually is diffuse, having total bodily involvement like fear, or cues that we learn to pick up, such as, if you see the rear end of a horse sticking out from a barn door, you automatically assume that there is a front end up there somewhere. These would be the kinds of general, impressional things that we learn very early in life.

Stimulus-response learning is motor learning and is mainly an operant behavioral type of response. A precise response to a discrete stimulus is acquired. *Response learning* often does not require repetition to be effective. One simply likes something or not. More dramatically, when one touches a hot stove, the learning is immediate. It takes only one mouthful for the young child to discover he does not like spinach, and many years may pass before he is willing to try again, only to discover that finally it is palatable, if not downright good!

The *chaining,* which is the second level in this model and the third in Gagné's more recent list (1965), is simply putting together a series of two or more stimulus-response connections. An example would be that to learn to see, the eye must learn to respond to light stimuli. The eye itself has to learn to stimulate the nerve endings and send the message back to the brain. The brain itself has to learn to integrate and interpret that particular message. This is the chain effect of the gradual growth of a number of internal responses to stimuli of the external world. Chaining behavior is evidenced in the treatment setting when a patient who has previously tolerated only the music moves into a group situation.

Type	Paradigm*	Description	Example
Response learning	S-R	Establishment of a response-connection to a stimulus specified along physical dimensions.	Contact with fire (S) elicits startle movement (R).
Chaining	S-R ～ S-R	Establishment of chains of response-connections.	Above paradigm is chained to presentation of heat (S), which elicits withdrawal (R).
Verbal learning (paired-associates)	S-r ～～～[s-R]	Establishment of labeling responses to stimuli varying physically within limits of primary stimulus generalization. Previous "response learning" assumed (as indicated by brackets).	Contact with fire (S) is associated with feeling of heat (r) and word hot (R) (association of heat sensation as s with word hot as R assumed).
Concept learning	S-r～～～s ⟶ Concept (three lines)	Establishment of mediating response to stimuli which differ from each other physically ("classifying").	Association of fire (S), steam (S), and hot metal (S) with feeling of heat (r) leads to association of heat with concept hotness.
Principle learning	—Concept, —Concept ⟶ Rule	Establishment of a process which functions like a rule "If A, then B," where A and B are concepts.	Concepts hotness and sharpness (similar paradigms assumed) lead to rule: "If hot or sharp, then painful."
Problem-solving	—Rule, —Rule ⟶ Higher order rule	Establishment of a process which "combines" two or more previously learned rules in a "higher-order rule."	Solving "if water boils at 212°F, at what C does it boil, given F=9/5C+32?."

*The paradigms shown have been designed to depict what is learned, and not the learning situation which leads to this result. In addition, it may be noted that beginning with concept learning, only the central portions of the inferred chains are shown.

Figure 1. Gagné's suggested ordering of the types of human learning (1964). Adapted by Klausmeier and Goodwin (1966, p. 263). Copyright 1966 by H. Klausmeier and W. Goodwin. Reprinted with permission.

For Gagné, *verbal learning* is a special type of learning because man's capacity for language permits internal links to be selected from his vocabulary storehouse. Every sound we make chains into groups of internal *s-r*'s to become words. Chains of larger groups become sentences, and so on. In his more recent list, Gagné added yet another learning dimension, *multiple discrimination*, placing it after *verbal learning*. This means that to learn something—to come to a concept—one must have experiences in sufficient quantity with a similar type of situation. For example, to come to the conclusion of the concept of appleness, we must first experience red apples, green apples, large apples, apple pie—all of the ways the word "apple" is used—until a full-fledged concept emerges. We learn to recognize classes and concepts by combining things under known similarities and discounting the differences. It can be shown, in a way, that no two things are ever identical.

When we finally have met enough stimuli of different but somewhat similar kinds, we can begin to make discriminations and come to the concept of the sameness, which leads us to the level of saying apples, fruit, so on—all of the things which we can name but which really do not exist. This is *concept learning*. The treeness does not exist. There exist many individual trees. In a sense, "forest" does not exist except in the abstract. Individual trees do make a forest, and when lumped together, the collection of trees is called a forest. However, "forest" as a "thingness" has a somewhat shady existence. Many words, such as "time-out," "socially acceptable behavior," "shaping," which we get caught up with when describing behavior, are shady words and really do not have too much relationship to reality, whatever that reality is at a given moment in history.

Gagné defines the next level, which is *principle learning*, as a chaining of two or more concepts. Water will boil when heated to 212°F. The concept of water boiling plus the concept of temperature produces a rule or principle type learning.

Problem-solving for Gagné seems to be the highest level of learning. This is another chaining pattern of combining learning from lower levels, but with an added requirement—thinking. The ability to think allows the individual to combine known principles into new ones and discover something new to him and possibly to the entire world.

One thing he does not discuss at any length is the area of creativity. I believe the reason many learning theorists shy away from the subject is that they are operating under the old-model impressions that state one is born with creativity whereas one can be taught cognitive information. We are now beginning to understand that creativity, like anything else, is teachable on the same level as other types of learning. However, what takes place is harder to describe. For my notion, creativity takes place at the *multiple discrimination* level of learning. The creative person when meeting the multi-stimulations that normally should result in a concept of similarity, also notices all of the differences. Therefore, he might combine chains of information differently and come out with a totally new classification or idea. Combining the old in a new way, or coming up with new ideas and manipulating them in an old way is essential to creativity. I will discuss this further in the section "Creativity as a Model for Thinking," beginning on page 68.

Although I categorize this figure as a model of sorts, it does not graphically describe the theory upon which it is built as easily as a model should. You still must go through the process of reading the descriptions and examples, letting each word visually plant itself in your mind, and then determining if you receive that same picture as the author intended. An exception would be the *paradigms,* which permit a more instantaneous grasp of understanding and thus fulfill a basic requirement for models.

Structure-of-Intellect Model

A classic example of a model is the Structure-of-Intellect (SI) model in Figure 2 developed by [the late] J. P. Guilford (1967) in 1958. It was derived in direct response to the single factor theory of intelligence. Guilford was a psychometrist, a factor analyst, who breaks things apart with statistics. He believed that the standard intelligence tests did not equitably measure intelligence. They tested how well one learned to read limited kinds of material only, and how to respond to those materials. The full dimensions of intelligence were not tested. Some people may have scored 140 on a highly respected intelligence test, yet may be unable to properly plant a seed in the earth or build a shed that would stand up. There are many dimensions of intelligence. The SI graphic (see Figure 2) is placed immediately before Klausmeier and Goodwin's design of Guilford's model (see Figure 3) in order to facilitate the reader's ability to compare the two.

Guilford concluded that intelligence is at least three-dimensional. To oversimplify a highly sophisticated process, to begin with there is something inside of you in that most complex of all machines known to man, the brain. You manipulate it in a variety of ways, which results in a change in behavior, otherwise known as using intelligence.

Guilford chose a morphological model because it could best treat the obvious parallels that occur between series of intellectual factors. He identifies three features of the intellect—there must be a *content,* a way we *operate*, and a resultant *product*. The *content* is further divided into four factors: *figural, semantic, symbolic, and behavioral. Operations* consist of five: *cognition, memory, divergent production, convergent production,* and *evaluation.* The *product* category breaks down into *units, classes, relations, systems, transformations,* and *implications.* A combination of one factor from each category produces an intellectual factor, or ability. This model implies that man can acquire intelligence in any number of 120 possible ways. That is, four *content* factors times five *operations* factors times six *products* factors equal 120 intellectual factors. Guilford's theory further reinforces the accepted concept that intelligence is not one-dimensional.

In the *content* category the *figural* factor is the most fascinating and meaningful to musicians. *Figural content* is concrete information experienced in the form of images directly through the senses. It is beyond definition and, in a sense, nonspecifiable because the moment you attempt to verbalize it, you are not speaking about what *figural content* is. *Figural* stimuli are simply what is going on out in front of us, and generally involves one or more sensory systems. It is at this figural, nonverbal level where the musical experience occurs, and this is the reason it is so hard to verbalize about the meaning of music.

Once we give something a name and let a symbol stand for it, like the letter "a," or an arrow pointing in some direction, we are at the *symbolic* level. Symbols are the "thingness" of the representation to be used for other purposes. They are all of the pictures upon which we place meaning. In music, these are expressed through the notation. Of course, the *semantic* level is the act of putting information into verbal form. At the *symbolic* and *semantic* levels we are introducing, in a sense, the scientific and analytical levels of our musical vocation—history, theory, and notation.

Finally, at the *behavioral* level the sociology of music and the humanities occur. The use of the term "behavioral" has created problems because of the mental images that word conjures in the mind. Guilford thinks of it strictly as learning of a social intelligence nature. That is, one learns how to function in one's environment in a socialized way. It is not behavioral in the sense of behavioral objectives or behaviorism. There is a hierarchy intended when behavior is described in this manner. One must understand figures before one can understand words, and one must have word knowledge and verbal understanding before it is possible to behave appropriately in society. The only real experiences implied for me in this category occur at the *figural* level. The remainder of the factors concern what we do by the process of abstraction.

At the *operations* category most of our formal education is centered around *cognition*—used in a more limited sense by Guilford (1967) to mean recognizing the information in the environment, rather than in its traditional meaning which covers all intellectual abilities—*memory*, and some *convergent thinking*—getting the one right answer. Schumacher (1977) would call this "dead" thinking because once the answer has been found, the problem is no longer interesting. "A solved problem is a dead problem. To make use of the solution does not require any higher faculties or abilities . . . the work is done" (p. 125). However, we should not consider that *convergent thinking* is wasted effort, because "it relates to what remains after life, consciousness, and self-awareness have already been eliminated" (p. 126). *Divergent thinking* involves creative thinking, and relates to arriving at many different solutions to a given problem. It is difficult to grade because if any answer can count, how do you differentiate between a correct and incorrect answer? Finally, we *evaluate* by making individual judgments about the decisions that have been reached.

The word "processes" is substituted for *operations* by some psychometricians in their interpretation of this category. Another semantic distinction is made by Guilford in his preference for the word "production" rather than "thinking," in reference to *divergent* and *convergent* operations. These examples point up the problem of effective communication through language.

The first four levels of the *products* category are simply super-impositions of integrating higher- and higher-order abstractions from the single entity, the *unit*, to organized masses of information, the *systems* level. The *unit* is the *only* product experience that is real. For instance, there is no such thing as apples; there is only a single apple. You have to show me one apple, then show me two, and we will call them apples. But the process required to call them apples is merely a cognitive experience. The minute we conceive of appleness, we have created a nonexistent entity, except for its existence in the human mind. When we think about relationships, then, there are relations which only can function through the mind, so to speak. They are non-real. We make them real if we are able to design an appropriate system. Of course, apples belong to the class we have identified as "fruit."

An even more striking example of the *unit* is the word "man." "There do not exist numbers of 'man,'" Rudolph Jordan (1951) declares, "but only individual men . . ." (p. 269). Singular and plural tenses have been reversed in this example, but the concept is not altered. "Numbers of men" are unreal, just as are "apples," and only exist through the mind. Reality resides in a single man or person, and relationships arise from the encounter of one single individual with another. This is important to understand in group music therapy.

A *relation* is a connection between two things. Then *systems*. *Transformation,* for Guilford, is the notion of taking from one kind of presentation and modifying or changing the form of the idea into another form, for example, visual to auditory. I would place modeling at this level.

Musical transposition is a special limited example of *transformation,* although this is in the auditory realm only. Another example would be transferring the sounds of some other medium—nature, for example—to musical instruments. Or, an idea or painting is expressed through a musical composition. The form of the product is being changed from one expressive mode to another. Finally, *implications* are the products resulting from the highest level of evaluation. It is the expectancy or prediction that one item of information will lead to another and, in that sense, is the connection between the two. To assist our accurate interpretation of Guilford's terminology, he says that the word "conception" is an appropriate synonym for the category termed *product*.

Klausmeier and Goodwin (1966) brought further meaning to Guilford's cube-shaped model by expanding it to include the results of learning, using a schematic arrangement (see Figure 3). With the addition of this category, which Klausmeier labels as *outcome*, this arrangement thus shows intellectual abilities as a developmental process. For the purpose of determining educational objectives, he states that Guilford's "concept of abilities is most meaningful when combined with outcomes of learning and broad subject-matter fields" (Klausmeier & Goodwin, 1966, p. 41). Of particular interest to us, Klausmeier has identified music as an outcome of the ability to think productively with nonverbal figural materials, which in the Structure-of Intellect model appears as the *figural content* level.

The only element that is missing in both the SI and Klausmeier models is the sensory category of intellectual abilities. With this additional element, a new equation emerges that is based upon the possibility that humans can be intelligent 120 ways in each sensory area because of the way we receive information. That is, there are 120 visual ways of being intelligent, 120 auditory ways, 120 tactile ways, 120 olfactory ways, and so on.[1] We are not intelligent in only one or several ways. We have different intelligence settings.

So far, over eighty tests have been identified which are supposedly factorially separate. That is, the test does not seem to relate to any of the other combinations of factors in the SI model. Only a very small number employ auditory stimuli, however. They all are visually oriented tests. It is possible that the general absence of recognition among intelligence specialists of sensory input as a factor of intelligence has contributed to the gradual decline in intelligence of the general population, as measured by standard intelligence tests.

Possibly this lack of understanding of sensory intelligence is an argument that we are now returning to the more right-brained days of Plato, Aristotle, and Socrates with its specialized attention to feelings, instantaneous thoughts, insights, intuitions. This is implied by one philosopher, Ervin Laszlo (1972), who gained international acclaim as a teenage concert pianist, turning to philosophy in his mid-twenties. He has had great impact on many areas of inquiry in the world today, principal among which is a general systems approach to world order. General systems theory holds that all phenomena in any system are interrelated and

---

[1] Employing Sears' formula, each of the five primary senses paired with a Structure-of-Intellect factor times one another would total 24,883,200,000 ways the integrated sensory self could manifest itself intellectually.

interdependent to the extent that cause and effect cannot be separated. A single variable can be *both* cause and effect (Laszlo, 1972).

Marilyn Ferguson (1980) further states, "Reality will not be still. And it cannot be taken apart! You cannot understand a cell, a rat, a brain structure, a family, or a culture if you isolate it from its context. *Relationship is everything*" (p. 157). If, indeed, Western culture is returning in its thoughts to the days of the ancient Greeks, there exists one advantage over the mystical philosophies of that early period in that now we have specified systems which have the capabilities to scientifically validate our particular theories.

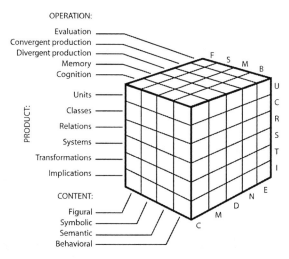

Letters on three edges of cube represent first letter of respective factor. However, in two instances this is not followed, i.e., in *content* category, M denotes *semantic* factor; in *operations* category, N stands for *convergent production*. It is presumed the author made these changes to avoid duplication of the first letter of factors in these two categories.

Figure 2. Structure-of-intellect model. Guilford (1967, p. 63). Copyright 1967 by McGraw-Hill. Reprinted with permission.

"The supreme challenge of our age," Laszlo (1972) says, "is to specify, *and learn to respect,* the objective norms of existence within the complex and delicately balanced hierarchic order that is both in us and about us" (p. 120). He claims that it is the only way a humanistic culture will come about. His model for the future is somewhat symbolic of

Guilford's *figural* level. That is, *figural content* is not expressible in words. It can only stand for itself. It encompasses the things, the feelings in our universes. We will meet Laszlo and his model later in this chapter in the section "Emergent Geopolitical Systems."

Research has shown that it is quite difficult for most persons to learn and memorize more than seven units of information at the same time. We tend to be unable to grasp anything that exists in more than seven discrete elements. A telephone number would be an example of the normal limits of this ability. It is presumably physiologically and neurologically impossible for most human beings to memorize, for example, twelve discrete units of information time after time. Thus, we are forced to reorganize our learning into clumps. Modeling is one way to produce some significant sized clumps.

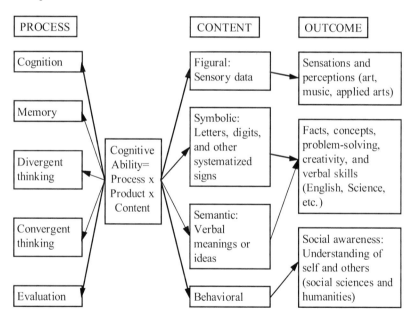

Figure 3. Cognitive abilities and learning outcomes based on Guilford (1959). Adapted by Klausmeier and Goodwin (1966, p. 42). Copyright 1966 by H. Klausmeier and W. Goodwin. Reprinted with permission.

After practicing at the piano so long, one no longer reads note by note, but rather in patterns. One no longer thinks in terms of individual notes. It is impossible. It is even neurologically impossible to read individual sixteenth notes at about 90 quarter note beats per minute and faster. One cannot read and respond to each note that fast. So one must read groupings. If an exception to the pattern occurs, for example, a D# occurring in a C major scale passage, the musculature has to receive a signal that alerts one to this. Thus, our notation system takes on models.

If somebody had told me this when I first began studying piano, I would have realized why I should practice my scales and arpeggios, knowing that later on I would simply think of a model and be able to rip off a scale passage with great agility. But I did not understand that, so I am a note reader. I start at the bottom of a chord or the beginning of a scale passage, get one finger right, put the next finger on, and so forth. It was unfortunate to only discover this so much later in life.

Relation Between Learning Theories and Man's Actional Nature

Often, we do not consider the basic assumptions behind whatever approach we are using. From a book titled *Learning Theories for Teachers*, the author, Morris Bigge (1971), points out that each learning theory or type of therapy has had its foundation in certain assumptions about the relationships of the organism man to the environment. The word "man" is used here in its generic sense. Bigge's thesis is displayed well in model form (see Figure 4).

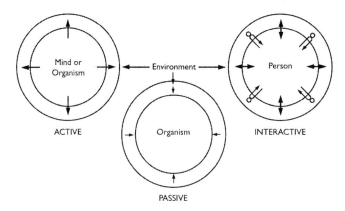

Figure 4. Man's actional nature. Bigge (1971, p. 16). Copyright 1971 by Bigge. Adapted with permission.

The model illustrates three assumptions pertinent to man's *actional nature*. Bigge identifies man's psychological nature as being *active, passive,* or *interactive.* In the first model, the person or the organism is *active* and is always working *at* the environment. Psychological developments come from within the individual, with the environment only providing a location for their natural unfoldment. In the middle example, the organism or person is *passive* and everything is acting *upon* him. The third model is one of *interactiveness* in that both the environment is working on the person and the person is working on the environment. The individual's reality is the product of his own unique and personal experience.

By Bigge's analysis, there is no single basic nature of man, but rather several which are based upon distinctly different and mutually opposed assumptions. This is one of the reasons I take issue with behavior modification as the primary treatment technique, its basic assumption seeming to be that man is a passive creature who is acted upon from the outside and then rewarded. The puzzle in this type of assumption is how do some people come to be the modifiers while other people have to remain the modified? I have never quite figured that out.

The *interactive* nature seems to be the model to which most Gestalt-field theorists subscribe. The basic assumption is that man's psychological nature arises from the personal-environmental relationships he develops which continually feedback on each other.

What makes this model the excellent example that it is? At first glance, one is aware of the uncluttered appearance. It is not difficult to determine where to start in the process to comprehend what the model is trying to communicate. Bigge (1971) has intentionally kept words to a minimum, perhaps too much so because the distinction between "organism" and "person" may not immediately be discerned. The text does provide some clarity, but I must wonder when he affirms that "in a relativistic sense, an organism is an aspect of both the person and his environment. A person usually closely identifies his biological organism with himself. But he also sees his organism in another light as an important aspect of his environment" (p. 226). I believe, in a real sense—not simply a "relativistic" one—that "organism" is both somewhere within the person and out there in the environment. In the first instance, organism/person, I see this as another way to express the mind-body connection. As for the person/environment bond, it is more profound when we understand that environment in this sense knows no boundaries, that is, is non-local, and can be totally removed from the "object" or person initiating the contact. This knowledge could no longer be regarded as merely mystical or paranormal even by the purest of sciences—physics—with the discovery of Bell's theorem, which mathematically proved the existence of non-locality. To grossly oversimplify this theorem, events separated by any distance imaginable can be instantly connected. Not surprisingly, many physicists believe the theory to be only nonsense (see "Time, the Servant of Music," Chapter 6).

Only a few symbols are needed to explain the total concept of man's *actional nature*. The sum total of the model is a quick and comprehensive understanding of a most complex idea.

Creativity as a Model for Thinking

Interest in creativity has swelled significantly over the last several decades. It has produced an abundance of books and articles on the subject and a number of models crafted to understand the creative process and facilitate its development. A mathematical formula developed by Don Fabun (1969) is a fine example of a creativity model (see Figure 5). Mathematical formulas, in general, are models, although they are meaningful only to those knowledgeable in the world of mathematics. The Fabun model is an exception, however, for it does not immerse itself in that mysterious language.

The World of
$$A^n + B^n \leftrightarrow C!$$

- "A" and "B" represent two concepts established in the mind.
- "C" represents a new "thing."
- The arrow $\leftrightarrow$ represents or means "yields" or "produces." It is pointed at both ends to indicate that the process is reversible and thus applies to discovery also. Further, it reminds one of the change of "A" and "B" by the "effect" of having found "C."
- "C" yields A + B, applied science
- "n" means any form, number, condition, or other aspect of A and B.
- "!" emphasizes the originality, newness, surprise at the result—C.
- Implication: "Conditions" can be prepared for (teaching?) Creativity!

Figure 5. The creative process. Adapted from Fabun (1969, pp. 6–10).

The formula can be expanded into any number of terms, but as it appears here figure *A* represents a concept, and the superscript lowercase *n* stands for any number of conditions of that situation. B^n stands for any number of conditions of another concept. The significance of *n* is that *A* and *B* can be very complex phenomena as well as simple ideas. *n* also expresses, and this is a most imperative step in the creative experience, both pertinent and seemingly impertinent information.

The double-tipped arrow points forward to *C,* which is the creative result. It also points back, implying that after you are pleased with one creative result, it works back on your reconditioning of *A* and *B* a second time. You keep putting more and more ideas together in different ways, which then produce new "things." The exclamation point does not imply that it is factorial as mathematicians might know it. It does not mean every condition of 1 through 10. It merely stands for "Aha!"—the effect of surprise, which seems to occur at the end of a creative experience. An implication from this model is that conditions can be prepared for teaching creativity.

Seven steps are described by Fabun that make the formula work. I discovered that Fabun's "prescription" easily lent itself to a graphic model. Figure 6 is my conception of the *Seven Steps to Creativity*. To set the creative process in motion, an individual must *desire* to create something original. Then follows *preparation,* which may require research, experimentation, even daydreaming, or mere "exposure to experience." It is an analytical process, seeking "to make the strange familiar." Having gathered this material, the individual must next *manipulate* it in an attempt to find some new pattern, that is, "to make the familiar strange." Rarely does the solution come immediately, thus the problem is set aside. The unconscious continues to wrestle with it during this *incubation* period. An *intimation* that a solution is at hand eventually "wells up into the consciousness like the light before the dawn." When the new idea is *illuminated,* the experience can best be described as "Aha!" or "Eureka!" Finally, to *verify* its value, the new pattern is tested to see if it works.

Fabun (1969) cautions that not all of these steps can be found in each creative act, and that while this model displays the creative process in an orderly sequence, the "mechanism by which the sequence occurs is only partially understood" (pp. 9–15). The most important ingredients in the creative process may well be the external clutter and the internal chaos.

Rudolph Jordan (1951) stated that "Men do not think in logical terms. Men think predominantly in the elastic terms of analogy" (p. 267). The secret is to choose suitable analogies if sound thinking is to result. How similar then are the paths to critical thinking and creativity.

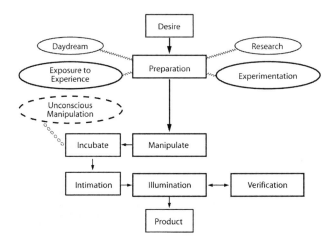

Figure 6. Seven steps to creativity. Adapted from Fabun (1969).

This creativity model coordinates quite remarkably with Guilford's Structure-of-Intellect model and Klausmeier's adaptation of it, as it logically should. In fact, Klausmeier identifies creativity as an expected outcome of the cognitive process. In viewing these four models (Guilford, Klausmeier, two by Fabun) side by side, yet another value of models emerges—the design of a totally new and different model by comparing existing ones. Is this not another example of a basic creativity precept—to make the familiar strange?

Five Stages of Development of Western Man

With the next three models we reach a rather sophisticated philosophical level of thinking. These models are based upon Gaston Bachelard's (1940) *epistemological profile* of the five stages of the cultural development of Western man. Bachelard (1884–1962), a French philosophy professor and prolific writer, also earned degrees in physics and mathematics. Thus, it should be no surprise that much of his work settled around the history and philosophy of science, although his attention to psychoanalysis and literary criticism might appear a bit on the outer edge. The relational character of the three models is intended to show that individual models can be linked together informally to expand thinking capabilities even further.

Bachelard's *epistemological profile* was informed by Alfred Korzybski's theory of time-binding (see "Semantic and Existential Implications for Music Therapy," Chapter 7). Time-binding asserts that human beings have the capacity to cumulatively add to their brain power from preceding generations, a power allegedly not available to animals and other lower-level beings. One difference in Bachelard's profile that is not found among other scholars is the use of the descriptor "Western." Bachelard was particularly conscious of different social and technological phenomena among cultures, but chose to incorporate Western man only into this system. Whether the absence of other cultures that exist around the globe has affected the profile's integrity can only be speculated. The concept of cultural development is important to us as a thinking tool, hence another reason to include this model in this paper. J. Samuel Bois (1966) interpreted Bachelard's profile in a lengthy text, which I have summarized in Table 1.

In the course of human history Western man has taken a number of semantic leaps, as symbolized by Korzybski's time-binding theory, which have forever altered his perception of his world. This model identifies five levels, or stages, each representing a distinct level of human evolution. After each leap, man became different from his former self. Bachelard saw that individual man is a microcosm of the total system, moving from the first to, hopefully, the fifth stage through the course of his lifetime. Of course, not all of us reach this full maturity, or, at best, achieve it in only some areas of our lives.

At the *sensing* stage man takes his feelings and sensations as an accurate indicator of what the world is like. This first stage is a holdover from primitive bicameral days when man did not question his feelings. These came from the gods, and were interpreted by high priests who held full sway over religious rites, and mystics who practiced their magic with full authority. It was a right-brained world. As a result, man's early writings were in poetry form—the language of the gods—which, incidentally, is also a form of music. This makes the usefulness of our field that much more evident.

Table 1
Five Stages of Development of Western Man

Sensing Stage—cause is not a question
- Feeling, not thinking
- Feelings are unquestioned, uncontrolled, self-justified
- Evaluative reactions—good-bad, like-dislike, beautiful-ugly
- Gods and spirits, superstitions, good luck charms, astrology, holy medals
- The world is what it *feels* like
- Objectivity not a question
- Man subject to whims of nature and one another
- Child—"me cookie," "me water," "me milk"
- Adult—"me pleasure," "me money," "me power," "me sex"

Classifying Stage—single cause
- Objectivity
- "Things" are, things separate, "real" substances and qualities, naming things, out-there world
- Verbal nouns, substantives, adjectives, verbs, adverbs
- Two-valued, opposites—yes, no, logic, single causes
- Aristotelian thinking, statistics good example
- Man can learn the real nature of things
- Things are what language says they are
- Only a good memory is necessary in a static world
- Self-defensive, dogmatic, rigid ideas

Relating Stage—multiple causes
- *What* things do and *how* they do it, things related
- Systematic observation
- Man is part of out-thereness, responds as science says
- Language of mathematical formulas
- Authority questioned, dynamic universe, complex parts
- Computer gods
- Man detached observer, can learn what nature is and how it works
- Machines multiply man's powers, new breeds of animals and plants
- Age of Science (with a capital S)
- Technology almost equals science
- Adaptive change and ideas

Postulating Stage—multiple causes plus self
- Man's awareness of self-reflexiveness
- "Objectivity" changes, rational absolutes crumble, limits of reason and rationality reached
- Era of "humble uncertainty"
- Prediction changes to possibility
- Multivalued, mathematics does not deal with nature, but with our knowledge and manner of relating to nature
- Question now becomes, "Shat can we *say* about nature?"
- Language becomes central again
- No set beliefs, man-made structure of postulates accepted as assumptions
- Self-evident truths, axioms, Aristotelian logic all disappear, dichotomies fade away
- Contradictions are acceptable
- Man in continual transaction with the world
- Man can change not only what he thinks but how (methods) he thinks—self-reflexiveness

Unifying Stage—systems relations
- Most genuine experience man can have
- Choice and awareness possible, man becomes conscious of his participation in flow of life
- At one with cosmic force, cosmic consciousness
- Living is feeling (passion)
- Transcends rationalized thinking, stands by itself as an experience
- Creative intuition, inspiration, supraconscious, enlightenment, transformation
- Unifies what culture sees as separated in contrast to divisive experience of strict objectivity
- Source of greatest human achievements and discoveries in all fields
- Man takes risk of living

Based upon Bois' (1966), chaps. 5, 6, adaptation of Bachelard (1973).

Many of us operate for much of our lives at this first stage. I think the significant statements in the model are the last two factors. When the child says, "me cookie," "me water," "me milk," he is operating at the *sensing* stage. He and the cookie and so forth are not too indistinguishable, so far as we know. His sense need becomes his actual need. Later in adulthood that behavior is changed to "me pleasure," "me money," and so on.

Objectivity is introduced in the second stage, the *classifying* stage, and thus was the beginning of science and philosophy. At this stage man can identify only a single cause to obtain the truth he seeks. The universe is static and can be explained only in black or white, right or wrong, good or evil.

Our present scientific attitude is somewhat stagnated at the *classifying* stage, for in science we can name, divide into parts, and measure by numerical figures. However, such methods are no longer viable, if, indeed, they ever were. To believe that we can cut something up into parts in order to understand its structure has led to all kinds of false and dead-end roads. A current contention of some scholars is that one cannot even begin to describe what something is by naming its parts. One can never arrive at the gestalt because not only does each part change in its environment with the other parts, but each continues to modify one another. The gestalt, thus, is something *quite different* from the sum of its parts. It is not more than, just different.

If we were to apply this theory to music and look at music history, for instance, as systems philosophy might look at it, we could then accept that there is a universe called "music" as the overall system. Then, there are the special compartments of baroque, classical, pop, folk, ethnic, and so on.

We may know of people who function under this particular type of fixed, two-valued thinking which exemplifies the *classifying* stage. In fact, all humans succumb to this level at times, as well we should. Objectivity and classifying are necessary thinking tools, but they have their limitations. Yet we only have reached stage two of the five stages of this concept of Western man's development.

The age of science is exemplified by the third stage, *relating*. It recognizes that the world is dynamic, in which there are multiple causes for a single phenomenon. The semantic leap to this stage was from a subject-predicate style language to the purity of mathematical thinking.

Multiple causes plus self emerge at the fourth level, the *postulating* stage. The realization occurs that we as participants in the situation are just as important as anything that we can extract from the objective world to observe. The fact that we pick a certain object to observe is a self-determined observation or abstraction, and we are responsible for making that observation or abstraction. Man is not a detached observer, but instead, an active participant in the dynamic processes of the world. To music therapists, this is the most important stage because it adds self to the multiple causes of stage 3, *relating*.

At the *postulating* stage "objectivity" changes, and we come to the realization that what we claim has been objective is a mirror of ourselves looking at the world, not the reality out there. This awareness is "self-reflexiveness." It was the discovery of this power that produced the semantic leap into this fourth stage of man's development, and seems to be one of the major differences between man and animal. Note that I say, "seems to be." We do not know. The dolphin is beginning to teach us something. If we continue to study it and other animals in their natural habitats, we may discover that self-reflexivity is not a solely human quality.

Self-reflexivity is a quality most of us are not conscious we possess: the idea that we are responsible for our behavior and our thoughts, that we can know that we are responsible, and that we are responsible for knowing that we are responsible. It always works back as self-reflexion. Any observations we make reflect as much of our individual selves as whatever is being observed.

However, most of us deal with the world at one of the lower levels. The world is as we see it. We take seeing as believing, making *that* the objective reality, not realizing that our very seeing has been affected by our past upbringing, and that what we see is not necessarily what is out there. We pick out what we *want* to look at, but it is, in a sense, no more objective than looking inside ourselves and asking, "What am I feeling or thinking?" We have yet to convince people that these behaviors and objective experimentation are both the same kinds of data.

Finally, the *unifying* stage brings it all together. Man is aware of his oneness with the cosmic process and of the interrelationships among all the systems which operate in the world. It is at this fifth stage that creativity is unfettered from the confining boundaries imposed by the first four stages.

Is the *unifying* stage an ideal which bears no relation to man's actual cultural development? Bois thinks not. But perhaps it appears beyond our comprehension because the semantic leap man must make into the *unifying* stage has not yet been completed. Could it be that [21st] century Western man is in the throes of that leap? It is rather significant that the first stage of man, *sensing,* and the *unifying* stage are absent from models of other scholars.

Editor's Note: Can any weaknesses be found in Bachelard's *epistemological profile* because he restricted his study to "Western" man? I believe comparing the "Five Stages of Development of Western Man" with the "Five Methods of Knowledge," the fundamental belief system of the Zuni American Indians of New Mexico, may be revealing. These "methods" were expressed in *Masked Gods,* the expansive study of southwestern indigenous (native) cultures, by Frank Waters, himself a product of the southwest United States. Below are the basic elements of these two systems in juxtaposition to one another.

Zuni: Five Methods of Knowledge	Bois: Fives Stages of Western Man
Geographic: Places, Rivers, Mountains, etc.	Sensing
Acquaintances: Persons, Animals, Objects	Classifying
Behavior(al): Learn, Think, Act, Speak	Relating
Acquired: Understanding	Postulating
Abstract Understanding: Intuitive, Self-evident	Unifying

You will note that the verbal descriptions found in Table 1 show similarities with the Zuni "methods of knowledge." The simple fact that both systems profess to five levels of development is more than coincidental, in my view.

The Zuni "*abstract understanding*" method and Bois' *unifying stage* may serve as an appropriate example of commonalities between the two. Waters (1950) explains that this level (method) is not an acquired understanding but is born in one. Whether it lies dormant and unused rather than awakened and strengthened rests with the individual. Bois employs such attributes as man's most genuine experience, creativity, enlightenment, passion, and cosmic consciousness to describe the *unifying stage*.

This one example is no attempt to assert that people in all cultures think and behave alike, but rather to take note of the possibility. Perhaps, had Bachelard expanded his outstanding profile to include societies outside the "West," we might be closer to an answer.

Patterns of Structural Thinking
Mental Models

Bois (1966) went further in the model-building process by organizing Kenneth Boulding's (1956) general patterns of structural thinking into seven basic mental models. I find that this hierarchical system lends itself well to a pyramidal design. Figure 7 is my conception of what that looks like.

This model, which is a composite of seven individual structural thinking tools, consists of empirical systems upon which mental models have been designed. As I have organized the model, the primary title of each level is a descriptor of an empirical system, e.g., *Framework,* and the subtitle, which immediately follows, is the corresponding mental model, e.g., *static structure.*

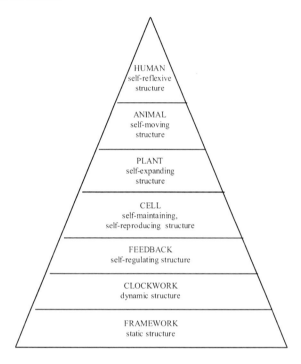

Figure 7. Empirical systems and corresponding mental models. Based upon Bois' (1966, pp. 138–155) adaptation of Boulding (1956).

The first empirical system is a static *framework* level in which we name things. This type of thinking belongs to Bois' (1966) *classifying* stage in the previous model, "Five Stages of Development of Western Man." With the *clockwork* system, another dimension is added—something works. The name is quite descriptive. One of the problems facing education today is that it is operating at this level, still applying classical science concepts and thinking in single cause modes. While clockwork is imperative in our high technology world, an educational system built on it cannot be a vehicle for acquiring knowledge.

The *feedback* system is the ultimate level at which most of science operates. Traces of living systems are evident at this level. Physiologically, humans and animals operate as feedback systems. When we are tired, our bodies insist on rest. When we engage in extreme exercise, our hearts beat faster, thus increasing circulation. Our bodies are constantly compensating to maintain a steady state. Likewise, at the psychological level corrections are made to achieve homeostasis. When the human system becomes overloaded and cannot make the necessary corrections, the result can be mental illness, substance abuse, or other behavioral abnormalities.

If our thinking is restricted to these first three levels, then we are content to confine ourselves to mechanical thinking when there are four still higher levels remaining. Most of us do not seem to know how to think past the *feedback* level. Bois (1966) states that while the mechanical systems are useful thinking systems, they lack the richness of the empirical world man deals with. "The world of humans lies beyond the world of mechanical models, cybernetics, operations research, or computers; it requires the use of mental models of the biological type . . ." (p. 146). The richer the models one regularly uses, the richer one's life will become.

With the next level, the *cell,* we move from mechanical to biological systems. Biological systems have four common requirements: (a) time to function and grow properly, (b) proper soil and climate, (c) adequate care and feeding, and (d) occasional pruning. Bois (1966) claims that all one really needs to know about these systems is contained in these brief instructions. The *cell* adds the idea of a self-maintaining system. It may be that some day the gap between the mechanistic *feedback* level and the organismic living *cell* level will be closed through greater knowledge of viruses. The virus seems to have the characteristics of a complex crystal when it is not on a host organism. When it finds a nice juicy living organism of some kind to attach itself to, it behaves like a living thing, and thus may be classified as half living and half static. It seems to have the property intermediate between so-called inanimate and animate objects. There is something in the middle that we do not know about.

The *plant* level contains all of the components of the previous levels and additionally advances them to a higher degree of complexity. The characteristic that distinguishes the plant from the cell is that all of the parts of the plant continue to differentiate themselves from the very beginning, even though they initially came from a unique "mother" cell. "It is an organization that is not put together by man, . . . [but rather] has grown according to a pattern buried in the chromosomes of its mother cell" (Bois, 1966, p. 149).

We come next to the *animal* system, and add yet another dimension—space-binding. That is, the animal can move in space when it wants to. It can go to where the water is, where the food is, flee from danger. The plant cannot.

Man is introduced at the seventh level—*human.* Seemingly, the difference between the human and the animal is not in man's language, but in the fact that man can be conscious that he knows that he knows. If I am using words in my head, I can become aware that I am doing so, and I can change those words to anything I care to. This is the same self-reflexiveness inherent in Bois' *postulating stage* (1966) in the "Five Stages of Development of Western Man" table. We tend to forget this idea of self-reflexivity much of the time. This level adds Korzybski's all-important time-binding factor, meaning that through words and symbols, man has the faculty to pass on his history and knowledge to the next person, the next generation. It does not have to be carried by the gene pattern or gene structure to the nervous system. Man knows he has a past, and is able to digest and summarize it with an aim toward projecting himself and his world into the future.

The factors of the *human* level produce a montage of a being—man—who has eliminated most threats to his happiness and survival. Most, that is, except for the greatest danger of all—himself. Man, particularly Western man, in his ultimate ignorance attempts to exert dominion over all he encounters, with little acknowledgement of this conceitful and destructive attitude. It is the ignorant conceit of man which speaks double-tongued that possibly something is greater than he, but acts as though that something is a greater "he." Yet this level is rich with possibilities, and should be the goal to which we all strive.

Looking at the evolutionary process, there are invertebrates, such as the planaria, which are able to regenerate a part that has been amputated. Maybe one of these days through mind power we will regain those parts we have lost over the ages. That is, we have probably sacrificed other devices that served us at a lower level of evolution in order to acquire this cerebrum we claim is so great. It may be possible one of these days to project oneself across time and space with the aid of nothing more than the mind. Then the victory of one man-made self-image over another will hold no allure, and man will have arrived at Bois' *unifying stage* (1966).

Everything has many dimensions, not just one or two. I offer the constructs of the *human* level to support my claim that alternative models are necessary, and that there should be as many models as there are readers of these words.

We now come to the last of Bois' three mental models, "Semantic Breeds of Men."

Semantic Breeds of Men

Bois (1970) extends the "Five Stages of Development of Western Man" to a classification system called "Semantic Breeds of Men," which is a profile of man's distinguishing character traits at each stage. All of man's behavior can be classified into these stages, which range from prehistoric times through "thinking and feeling at a transcendent level of experience" (p.

114). Each stage of this evolutionary process is identifiable by specific characteristics which, when grouped together, construct a discrete profile, or using Bois' term, a breed. Bois' purpose in devising this system is to sort out the types of thinking (breeds) and to develop methods for dealing with them.

"Breeds of Men" is displayed in Table 2. Like the "Five Stages of Development of Western Man" model (see Table 1), this is also a list of descriptors. So why should I bother to include another model whose shape has previously been demonstrated? There are several reasons. First, these models, as well as Boulding's "Empirical Systems and Corresponding Mental Models," (see Figure 7), show a progressive theory of development—each is built upon the preceding one. They are relational, and only by displaying all can the concept be completed.

Secondly, I challenge the reader to design yet a different model for one or both tables. All three models were originally presented by their creators in cursive format. I condensed them to a modified outline style. It required but little creativity to change Boulding's model to a more traditional design—a pyramid.

Thirdly, skeptics might challenge whether a table is a bona fide model. I believe it is because it compresses a lengthy concept into a brief, manageable order. This, as previously stated, is the strength of models.

There is yet another reason for covering this topic so thoroughly. The cultural development of man is as germane to music therapy as is the influence of music on behavior. We cannot ply our trade without a solid grounding in human behavior. Not many texts on this subject approach it from such a comprehensive and philosophical position. Now, I leave it to you, the reader, to carry model-building another step further.

Table 2
Breeds of Men Classification

Breed 1: *Primitives of All Times*
1. Unconsciously identify perceptions with "objective facts"
2. Interpret behavior of others by automatic projection of their own attitudes, purposes, and desires
3. Have a strong dose of affectivity that is taken as the measure of "objective truth" of what they are sure is going on
4. Are certain that nothing of importance or value is happening or has happened outside the world as they see it

Breed 2: *Classifiers*
1. Demand "exact" meanings of words

2. Tend to explain what happens in terms of the class in which they pigeonhole the happening
3. Tend to see the world as made up of opposites; thinking is often either-or
4. Tend to call people names (a rationalization of stage 1 thinking)
5. Tend to use unconscious confusion of interpretations and descriptions, or use value terms instead of plain report language
6. Rationalize their actions when contradicted; deny defensiveness, and expect no contradiction because they have the unexamined conviction that their statements are objective

Breed 3: *Relators*
1. Have improved methods of knowing the world about them by creating new language of mathematics
2. Swear by research and in the magic of quantity
3. Use mechanical thinking to understand and manipulate events and people
4. Change names of things without really changing the "thingness," as though it changed thought
5. Still believe that the "words" they use are the final say on how best to chop the world of ongoings into manageable chunks
6. Thinking is in terms of "cause and effect"
7. Make sharp distinction between theory and practice
8. Have not learned to live in space-time, but in a space— including things, persons, and events—that exists as a milieu from which they are somewhat independent

Breed 4: *Postulators*
1. Are self-actualizers, in (Abraham) Maslow's sense[2]
2. Are of a culture, know it, but are not locked into it
3. Are committed to definite philosophy of life possibly too rich to be easily formulated into simple statements that they can accept as adequate
4. Live in a broad space-time context where every human being has the right to feel at home and the duty to help satisfy the basic needs of others

---

[2] Maslow (1968), renowned for his crusade for a humanistic approach to psychology, placed self-actualization at the top of his famous "Hierarchy of Human Needs" system. One who seeks this need strives to fulfill his/her potential, and to be the most complete, fullest person possible, that is, "to be all that one can be."

5. Have grown beyond seeking only the satisfactions of their needs; make altruism their dominant passion

6. Have no bitterness toward those who oppose them, misunderstand them, or vent on them their dissatisfaction with life

7. Stand firm in their choice of what they have learned to evaluate as a better alternative with a calm readiness to face the consequences

8. Are aware that the use of discursive reason has its limitations; conclude that the next step in human evolution has to be at the affective level

9. Realize that at each moment of life humans are pushing themselves into the unknown, and thus they discount the absolute predictability value of statistical trends and do not rely on carefully planned rehearsals of future encounters or situations; realize that such predictions come from inside their heads and may change tomorrow

Breed 5: *Participants*

1. Theory of knowledge ceases to be a "general system of knowing;" it has broader scope and becomes the learned art of experiencing in an ever-growing awareness

2. To be at one with all processes—persons, things, situations— that share the universe; supersedes knowing what is and why it is

3. Rather than be guided by theories, they are led by binding force that holds universe together

4. Living is an art that blends together thinking and feeling at a transcendent level of experience

Adapted from Bois (1970, chaps. 7–13).

The world of *primitive man* was structured by his sensory experience. The way he perceived the world was the way he believed it to be. He and the world were alike. Many Breed 1 people are among us today, and it is for them—or us—that the television commercial producers fashion their messages.

Read the list of characteristics of this breed and you will observe that it well describes the world of the neurotic. Psychoanalytic theory assumes that Breed 1 is the normal human functioning level. "No wonder," Bois (1970) says, "that there is some magic left in many psychotherapeutic procedures in vogue today. It may well be that the main task is one of education and not of 'treatment.' If we could bring every individual to the level of cultural evolution that befits the present age of humankind, we might need fewer clinics and mental institutions" (p. 60).

Speech ushered in the new breed of man—the *classifiers*. While the world of words widened man's horizon to an almost overwhelming degree, that world became fixed by those words. The majority of us are still Breed 2. We read not to seek knowledge and understanding, but for status.

We sometimes say that the student has a concept if he can parrot back the definitions that have been given in class as the perceptual definitions. What is a melody? The student dutifully recites the answer that was given him to write down in his notebook, and so we assume he understands the concept. We then play a musical example and ask him to identify the melody, only to discover that he does not know what a melody is. The classifying level has been in operation here.

The *relators* can be identified by their concern for finding the "truth," which they believe to be static. Once they have discovered it, it becomes fixed in a world of its own outside space-time. The obsessive-compulsive individual who rigidly holds to a set of behaviors that are meaningful only to him is operating as a Breed 3.

Breed 4 has not yet been studied long enough for a profile to have been shaped. The list of traits in Table 2 is by no means complete, but merely suggestive of some typical characteristics. *Postulators* "are of a culture, know it, but are not locked into it" is the second characteristic in the list. There is a great distinction to be made between that and being aware that one is part of a culture but to be locked into it. At this level, the person has ways and means of removing himself from cultural influences if he chooses.

Breed 4 persons "are committed to a definite philosophy of life possibly too rich to be easily formulated into simple statements that they could accept as adequate," is their third characteristic. It becomes increasingly difficult to verbally describe one's feelings, that is, what that figural level *is* out there that we are actually sensing and knowing in certain ways. But we have yet to intellectualize it with the words that can express what that feeling is.

Breed 5, the *participants*, is less definitely described. It is interesting to note that Bois classifies musicians and artists of all types as *participants*. By "artists" he means those great individuals through the ages, such as Shakespeare, Walt Whitman, Beethoven, Mozart, who have really affected the lives and changed the thoughts of later generations. By insight, which is expressed through their art, they have predicted and foreseen the future. *Walden,* by Henry David Thoreau led to *Walden Two,* a work of science fiction by the late renowned behavioral psychologist B. F. Skinner (1948). The novel is set in a modern-day Utopia, Walden Two, where many of our contemporary values have been rendered obsolete. Through scientific technology of human conduct methods, human problems have been solved. The two "Waldens" came from basically different backgrounds, yet by some accounts, Skinner was influenced by Thoreau.

Participant people are those who, in a sense, accept a common meaning for the word "participate." They are participating at every moment of their lives. All around us we see what appears to be a demonstration of this in the numerous movements for awareness training. However, if you analyze what is going on, the person is training you to be aware, but is using methods based upon characteristics of these lower-level breeds. Lower-level methods are used to train one to operate at the highest level. Maybe it succeeds, but in all probability it does not.

Bois (1970) eloquently sums up the essence of Breed 5 by saying, "The experience of being at one in a felt symbiosis with things, people, and situations may be viewed as the initial phase of a new art, the art of participating with expanding awareness in the creative thrust of cosmic energy" (p. 126).

Being a general semanticist, Bois naturally drew a strong connection between man's nature and his language. Returning to the "Five Stages of Development of Western Man," words have been "invented" which express how man relates to himself at the specific stages. Bois has grouped some of these words into clusters or families—in a manner of speaking, capsulizing the history of the culture of language—each cluster being assigned to one of the stages of development, excepting stages 1 and 5. There are no words at Breed 1 of man's development because he is existing in a sensory environment. At Breed 2 objects are identified by their "form." That word implies permanence, a characteristic of this breed and the family of words associated with it. The word "self" is an apt example. Breed 3 words such as "self-improvement" show action. Breed 4 gives trans/formation; there is no concern about which is the first or which is the second action. It is the process that matters. "Self-renewal" is a Breed 4 word.

Breed 5 is also without language, for when one reaches that stage, one is a *participant,* and verbal language is no longer needed. Bois places poetry and the arts in the Breed-4 cluster. Although he does not mention music specifically, I believe he considers music to be a Breed-1 experience where there are no words, and at Breed-5 where one does not need words any longer.

The "Five Stages of Development of Western Man," the "Mental Models" (Empirical Systems and Corresponding Mental Models), and the "Breeds of Men" are hierarchical in so far that they signify man's historical development. Although each stage may be observed in the individual through the maturation process, progression is not automatic, nor must one experience everything at a lower level before moving up to higher ones. Different parts of the operating "self" function at different levels. Many people function at a high level technologically, but rarely, if ever, reach that same level psychologically. When describing the Mental Models in *The Art of Awareness,* Bois (1966) said that the skilled thinker will employ a broad mix of the models. The trick is to know which tool is most suitable for the task at hand.

Boulding (1956) explained that the attributes of each level of the Mental Models are accumulative to a degree in that each level contains characteristics from all the lower levels. Man is an accumulation of his history.

Emergent Geopolitical Systems

The final model I wish to offer is graphically quite different from what has been presented thus far. Titled "Emergent Geopolitical Systems," it is a systems concept of the history of man and the organization of geographical-geopolitical systems developed by Laszlo (1974). A systems approach is a method of looking at the world holistically in terms of sets of integrated relations. His theories on the worldview have created a lot of excitement outside the field of the philosophy of science, although his colleagues are somewhat less enthusiastic. He believes strongly in the value of visual graphics to explain a complex theory, and has liberally sprinkled his writings with original models. Figure 8 represents a general systems model of socioeconomic development. Laszlo's model further reinforces my theory that there exists a multiplicity of shapes and designs models can assume, and further that there is a "correct" model to serve a specific purpose only in so far as it meets the needs of the user.

Laszlo points out that the *emergent geopolitical systems* model departs from classical systems models, which tend to be horizontally conceived, that is, they show either a single sociopolitical system, or else a set of transacting systems existing in a similar state of development. However, such models do not account for the "vertical" shifts of societies, semantic leaps, if you will, that explain the historical progression from simple kinship societies to highly complex ones. The present model incorporates both the traditional self-stabilizing (Cybernetics I) and the equally important self-organizing (Cybernetics II) concepts.

Commencing at the bottom of the diagram with relatively simple and homogeneous societies—the family, the clan, and the tribe—it progresses upward to more complex and heterogeneous ones, the highest level being the *planetary system,* which consists of *federation of states* and *interstate organizations.*

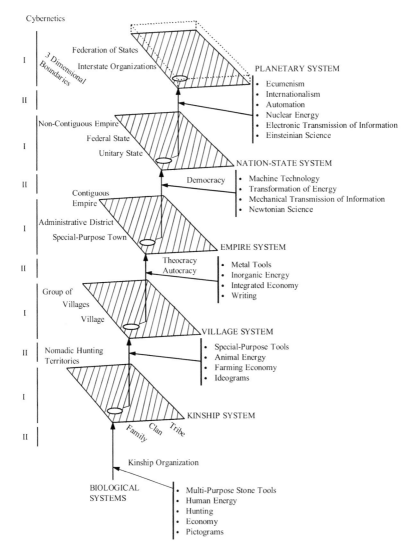

Figure 8. Emergent geopolitical systems. Laszlo (1974, p. 40). Copyright 1974 by Laszlo. Reprinted with permission.

This model makes specific use of the concepts of Cybernetics I and Cybernetics II, which are presented in the left column of the figure. These are present-day concepts based upon so-called feedback systems in

electronics. To explain, in electronics through negative feedback a fraction of the electrical output is returned to change the input in such a
way that the amplifier will have a near constant gain. For example, negative feedback cancels out the hum that is picked up from the 60-cycle vibrating current in all electric wires. Somewhere in the circuit the same 60-cycle signal is fed back into the input, but 180 degrees out of phase. If the signal is 180 degrees out of phase it will cancel itself out as it is coming in. Like an anechoic chamber, which absorbs the sound the moment it occurs, you hear little or nothing even though you are yelling at the top of your lungs. That is negative feedback.

In Laszlo's model, Cybernetics I is negative feedback and relates to a society's self-stabilizing level of development. This is the tendency of a sociocultural system to stabilize itself by creating laws, mores, customs, regulations, and higher degrees of organizational development. All societies reach this level at some point in their evolution. As a society evolves, it becomes more and more organized and makes more and more rules. Stability is maintained until somebody comes along—some mind, some change of nature—and punctures a hole in that negative feedback system, that regulatory system, and introduces new forms of societal organization that then proceed to evolve into a higher-level system. This *self-organizing* process of change to something different is called Cybernetics II, or positive feedback.

According to Laszlo (1974), Cybernetics I occurs both in primitive societies where any technologies which do exist are primarily biological and thus not subject to rapid changes in organization, and in highly developed societies, "where the culturally transmitted technologies have reached the limits of their operational effectiveness. By contrast, Cybernetics II operates [only] whenever new technologies are evolved in a sociocultural system" (p. 38).

The list of terms set off with vertical bars in the model are significant kinds of happenings, usually technological or scientific, which stimulate change and cause positive feedback to enter the system, thus accelerating the system to a higher level of organized complexity. The vertical arrows in the model signify that acceleration. This general systems interpretation of sociocultural evolution is derived from a study of everything from the atom up through all of the physiological mechanisms. The rule of the universe as expressed in this theory seems to be to develop higher and higher levels of organization. As some organizations disintegrate, others are in the process of being built. We can observe examples all around us of Laszlo's models, from the nuclear family unit all the way up to the governments of the superpowers.

There are some interesting comparisons to be made between this model and Bois' stages of man's development (see Table 1). The history of sociopolitical societies displays the same characteristics found in man's cultural development. The primitive *kinship system* is based on the same types of experiences as are found in Bois' *sensing stage*. Similar parallels can be drawn between the two models all the way up to Laszlo's *planetary system* and Bois' *unifying stage*.

The strength of models again is revealed through his example of relationship. How much easier it is to perceive with models that can be placed physically side-by-side.

One final statement needs amplification before we leave this model. The systems approach, like all theories, has certain commonalities, distinct features, and non-varying aspects that set it apart from other phenomena. Laszlo (1972) calls these *invariances of organization*. He goes on to identify the four basic organizational invariances of natural systems.

The technical definition of a natural system is an open system in a self-maintaining or steady-state. *Openness* applies to the steady exchange activities—intake and output—that are required to maintain the system in its dynamic steady-state. The weight of this strikes home when Laszlo (1972) asserts that, "Organisms are open systems all their life. They could not exist for more than a few minutes without the constant intake and output of energies, substances, and information" (p. 40). Music, an example of an open system, flows into the organism and then must move out. "Moving out" comes in many forms, but those which concern us most are characterized by intra- and interpersonal behaviors. "Natural," as Laszlo employs the term, contrasts with "artificial" and not with "social." His definition reads, "Any system which does not owe its existence to conscious human planning and execution [including man himself] is a natural system . . ." (p. 23).

Natural systems are wholes with irreducible properties is the first organizational invariance. By analogy, music, a corporate organization such as NAMT, and an organism such as the brain are systems. We cannot reduce them any further. They exist as wholes.

Second is *natural systems maintain themselves in a changing environment*. A system perpetuates itself and strives for homeostatic being, much as our bodies do. When the body is out of order, its own processes counter that by eating more or eating less, sleeping, releasing or inhibiting blood flow, and so on. There is a commonality in a system which allows it to adapt although the environment shifts.

The third invariance is *natural systems create themselves in response to the challenge of the environment*. The whole of organic evolution is built on the assumption that species will rise and fall as environmental conditions shift. Why did NAMT organize in the first place? Because, in order to effect change in our profession and gain acceptance from the health industry, we had to strengthen our professional growth and development.

As we interface with other social systems in our culture we will need to change to avoid extinction.

Finally, *natural systems are coordinating interfaces in nature's hierarchy*. "They are wholes in regard to their parts, and parts with respect to higher-level wholes" (Laszlo, 1972, p. 67). NAMT is multi-stratified and thus not dependent for survival on the individual passing through. Some people in the organization are dead and buried already. Some of us soon will be, and other people keep coming in to continue the cycle. Yet something called "NAMT" tends to continue because of its integrated hierarchical nature. Put another way, there cannot be a "me" without a "you." It is only the "you" that gives the "me" identity. "Me" and "you" are *coordinated interfaces*.

In summary, Laszlo (1972) states that "The systems view of nature is one of harmony and dynamic balance. Progress is triggered from below without determination from above, and is thus both definite and open-ended. To be 'with it' one must adapt, and that means moving along. There is freedom in choosing one's paths of progress, yet this freedom is bounded by the limits of compatibility with the dynamic structure of the whole" (p. 75). His model shows this very well.

Models can release creative energy, trigger thought processes, and open the mind to new possibilities. Whether one is engaged in examining the designs of others or creating one's own, the process seems to work. Yet there is another purpose that model-building serves, that being to create a deeper understanding of the subject matter. Of course, that should be obvious, as this chapter title states. However, it warrants further emphasis.

The examples presented were chosen not only for their graphic designs, but also for their concepts. The structure of the intellect, the development of Western man, and the systems view of the world all bear directly on music therapy. Indeed, we cannot hope to understand our discipline or function within it without an awareness of our own human species and the world about us. It is through intentional exposure to a wide variety of ideas that we are able to come to a reasonable understanding of a single field of knowledge. Alfred North Whitehead (1978), eminent 20th century philosopher, phrased it thusly:

> The true method of philosophical construction is to frame a scheme of ideas, the best that one can, and unflinchingly to explore the interpretation of experience in terms of that scheme. . . . All constructive thought, on the various topics of scientific interest, is dominated by some such scheme, unacknowledged, but no less influential in guiding the imagination. The importance of philosophy lies in its sustained effort to make such schemes explicit, and thereby capable of criticism and improvement. (p. xiv)

Whitehead was describing the philosophical method, but his statement applies equally well to the concept of modeling. It is a model that serves as a frame for any "scheme of ideas," and makes the ideas that emerge explicit and "capable of criticism and improvement." That is a definition worthy of Webster.

Models are the gateway to learning. We encounter them very early in life as toddlers through puzzles and building blocks. As we mature, our models become more sophisticated and complex, although not necessarily more meaningful or instructive. Economist Hazel Henderson made the startling statement, "any system that cannot be modeled cannot be managed" (Capra, 1988, p. 255). Model-building is a lifelong process. We need only to be aware of that fact (not to mention, Henderson's omen), and open ourselves more to the myriad uses this magnificent thinking tool holds for us.

Editor's Summary

Models drive the whole of society. Growth and development of human beings and technology occur only through the stimulus of models. Equally vital are thinking or mental models, models which help humans bring order to the thinking process. Language tends to create a static environment, freezing one's ability to "think outside the box." Freed from language constraints, mental models allow for openness and fluidity of thought.

A deceptively simple puzzle of 12 pieces, *Hexed*, demonstrated the complexity of models and what they can teach us. Creating musical compositions based upon a stimulus—abstract or concrete—from the environment showed that one's mental imagination can be stretched in unusual ways.

Examples of a variety of mental models created by well-respected scholars point up the credibility of model-building for thinking. One such example, Robert M. Gagné's *Types of Human Learning*, has been designed as a model by Klausmeier and Goodwin. It is a sequential, hierarchical patterning of the types of human learning. The "Structure-of-Intellect" model devised by J. P. Guilford was selected by Sears as the most appropriate model for expanding the "Processes in Music Therapy" (see Chapter 2). Guilford adopted a cube configuration for his model. Although on paper this shape cannot fully display the three-dimensional character inherent in a cube, nonetheless it does communicate the idea of intellectual learning. Placing the figure next to Klausmeier and Goodwin's adaptation of the cube model into a schematic design is meant to expand the reader's understanding of the value of models. Klausmeier and Goodwin also added another dimension to Guilford's three categories of intelligence *(content, operations, products),* that being *outcome.*

Three circles showing the basic actional relationships of man *(active, passive, interactive)* to his environment constituted a model by Morris Bigge which is visually quite simple and easy to grasp, confirming once again the advantage of models. Don Fabun's creative process, which is expressed in a brief mathematical formula, and his seven steps to creativity were easily adapted as models. Tables also make good models, particularly when the subject matter is lengthy and complex, such being the cases with Bois' "Five Stages of Development of Western Man" and "Semantic Breeds of Men," adapted from Gaston Bachelard's *epistemological profile.* The present author found that Boulding's "Empirical Systems and Corresponding Mental Models" lent itself well to a pyramidal form because of its hierarchical character.

The final model differs both in theme and structure. It is Ervin Laszlo's "Emergent Geopolitical Systems," which depicts man's history through the organization of geographical-geopolitical systems. Unlike other systems models, which are horizontally constructed, Laszlo created a vertical design, thereby opening a different concept for building models. Placing this model alongside other models sampled in this chapter reveals a relational character among models in general.

Models are the gateway to learning. From infancy on, they are all about us, influencing and determining our progress through life.

References

Bachelard, G. (1973). *La philosophie du mon; essai d'une philosophie du nouvel esprit scientifique.* Paris: Presses Universitaires de France.

Bigge, M. L. (1971). *Learning theories for teachers* (2nd Ed.). New York: Harper & Row.

Bois, J. S. (1966). *The art of awareness.* Dubuque, IA: Wm. C. Brown.

Bois, J. S. (1970). *Breeds of men.* New York: Harper & Row.

Boulding, K. E. (1956). *The image.* Ann Arbor, MI: The University of Michigan Press.

Brown, B. (1974). *New mind, new body.* New York: Harper & Row.

Capra, F. (1988). *Uncommon wisdom.* New York: Simon & Schuster.

de Bono, E. (1970). *Lateral thinking.* New York: Harper & Row.

Fabun, Don. (1969). *You and creativity.* Beverly Hills, CA: Glencoe Press.

Ferguson, M. (1980). *The Aquarian conspiracy.* Los Angeles: J. P. Tarcher.

Gagné, R. M. (1964). Problem-solving. In A. W. Melton (Ed.), *Categories of human learning.* New York: Academic Press.

Gagné, R. M. (1965). *The conditions of learning*. New York: Holt, Rinehart & Winston.

Guilford, J. P. (1959). Three faces of intellect. *American Psychologist, 14,* 469-479.

Guilford, J. P. (1967). *The nature of human intelligence*. New York: McGraw-Hill Book Co.

Johnson, W. (1965). *Verbal man: The enchantment of words*. New York: Collier Books.

Jordan, R. (1951). *The new perspective*. Chicago: University of Chicago Press.

Klausmeier, H. J. & Goodwin, W. (1966). *Learning and human abilities* (2nd ed.). New York: Harper & Row.

Kohner Brothers (1972). *Hexed* (a puzzle game). Thyne Games Division. East Patterson, NJ.

Laszlo, E. (1972). *The systems view of the world*. New York: George Braziller.

Laszlo, E. (1974). *A strategy for the future*. New York: George Braziller.

Maslow, A. (1968). *Toward a psychology of being*. Princeton: Van Nostrand.

Reese, Hayne W. (1971). The study of covert verbal and nonverbal mediation. In Alfred Jacobs and Lewis Saks (Eds.), *Psychology of private events*. New York: Academic Press.

Schumacher, E. F. (1977). *Guide for the perplexed*. New York: Harper & Row.

Skinner, B. F. (1948). *Walden two*. New York: Macmillan.

Stogdill, Ralph M. (1972). Introduction: The student and model-building. In Ralph M. Stogdill (Ed.), *The process of model-building in the behavioral sciences*. New York: W. W. Norton.

Waters, F. (1950). *Masked gods*. New York: Ballantine Books.

Whitehead, A. N. (1978). *Process and reality: An essay in cosmology*. Corrected edition by David R. Griffin and Donald W. Sherburne (Eds.). New York: The Free Press.

Chapter Four

On Music, Mind, Education, and Human Development

Children still have the capacity to be puzzled
[to wonder]. . . . But once they are through with the
process of education, most people lose the capacity of
wondering, of being surprised.

Erich Fromm

Our proficiencies have cost us
our capacity for wonder.

George Will

Editor's Introduction

This lecture was originally presented at the National Association for Music Therapy 28th annual conference, Anaheim, California, October 28, 1977. Sears' opening remarks in Anaheim were omitted in the course of adapting the lecture to the written page, for these were deemed to be more of a personal nature than seemed appropriate in a work of scholarly intent. Yet, in retrospect, they speak of Sears' "nature," and seem suitable to introduce the more serious and thought-provoking message that follows.

Here, then, are those initial statements. "I wish I had the humility of Dr. Albert Einstein when he appeared before a forum such as this and said, 'Ladies and gentlemen, I have nothing to say. When I do, I will be back.' And, of course, he did go back. Today I do have something to say to you. I would like to paraphrase the introduction of what I will offer you [which is borrowed from a Broadway musical]: Some curious and interesting things happened on the way to this forum . . . .

"Some months ago I had conceived of what I would say to you today as being strictly scholastic, strictly academic. . . . I was going to be well-prepared, even write out my speech to read to you. But that is not me, and all I really have to offer you is me. . . . I only ask that you hear and listen. Do not worry about who is speaking, or if it doesn't come true. Instead, listen to your own listening while I try to speak to you about some certain things I think are very vital, very important." Therefore, to paraphrase Sears, read and ponder what follows.

The World of Wonder

"Wonder" is a very important word to me. I think we should rename or substitute for the word "research" the word "re-wonder." Is there any activity in which "wonder" should be more soundly rooted than when one is engaged in research? This was what Wendell Johnson (1956) had in mind when he said, "all we gain from wonder by wonder is increased" (p. 146).

The English language employs some tricks which confuse the mind. For example, derivatives of root words often contradict or have little relation to the root. To illustrate, the word "rational" means having reasoning or understanding; standing for truth and logic. However, through the magic of our word system, by adding three little letters—"ize" to create the word "rationalize"—we change the word from truth to falsehood. In psychiatric terminology, to "rationalize" is to tell oneself the untruths which are supposed to force the truths.

The definition of "organism" is all but lost in the derivative, "organization." "Compromise" has distinctly different and conflicting meanings. To the British it has a positive flavor, meaning to come to mutual agreement over a disputed issue. In the United States it implies one has surrendered one's position through concession. One is supposedly weakened by compromise, thus the word carries negative implications. The same word or symbol may carry two or more different meanings, even to people who share the same culture. That is our different plays with words, with symbols, or with music.

The purpose of this chapter is to leave the reader wondering, but most importantly, to present something worth wondering about. When we cease to wonder, we leave philosophy. Experimental philosophy is wonder with implications for experimental testing. It is a bridge between pure wonder and empirical test. As Erich Fromm says in the quote which opens this chapter, children have the capacity to wonder, but that gift usually shuts down by the time adult status arrives. As we stand in awe and are filled with more and more wonder, perhaps we shall rediscover the "capacity to be puzzled" and to wonder, and then be able to make the leaps in our thoughts to arrive at a few "Aha's!"

How to and Not to Raise Children

When in a bookstore, I have discovered that books that mean the most to me were picked up with the right hand, transferred to the left hand, and put on the stack to be bought without so-called conscious consideration. Why that happens I do not know. I would like to talk about the meaning of one of those books I picked up with my right hand, *The Magical Child*, written by Joseph Chilton Pearce (1977). "Wonder," and a lot more, is the subject of *The Magical Child*. Pearce is also the author of such celebrated works about the human condition as *The Crack in the Cosmic Egg, Exploring the Crack in the Comic Egg,* and later works *Evolution's End* and *From Magical Child to Magical Teen*. The subtitle of *The Magical Child* is *Rediscovering Nature's Plan for Our Children,* which is very revealing about Pearce's philosophy.

In this book, Pearce puts forth a comprehensive view encompassing a number of very broad generalizations. Anyone who tries to take a comprehensive view leaves out many details—a number of small particulars that some people in science and research regard as specifics. He begins with the notion that each of us is a hologram of a universe, or of universes.

Holography is a method of lenseless photography. When a coherent light beam, such as from a laser, is passed through the photographic plate upon which an image has been photographed, a three-dimensional image appears. The most remarkable feature is that when *any piece* of the hologram is illuminated with coherent light, the entire original image is reconstructed. When a hologram is cut in two and projected again, the entire original image is contained in each half. Cut these pieces and again each piece will produce the entire image. This process can be repeated over and over, and while the image will become fuzzy as the pieces get smaller, the complete picture will always be projected.

Dennis Gabor discovered the mathematical principle of holography in 1947, for which he was later awarded the Nobel Prize. However, it was not until 1965, with the invention of the laser beam, that holograms were first constructed (See "A New Perspective on Reality" in Wilber, 1982).

Thus, each of us mirrors the total means of our universe. The only problem has been that in our Western culture practices of childbirth and child rearing, the holographic process seems to have been canceled out. With the idea that we are all individually reproducing a picture of the universe, Pearce uses the term "bonding." It is not the same use of the word as in the stimulus-response bond theory of learning. "Bonding" merely means that we are bound to certain tangibles in our lives. The first and most important person we become bound to, of course, is our mother.

Bonding is expressed in a variety of ways. Recently, during the first session of a music therapy clinical practicum, the students were asked to introduce themselves by telling where they were from—a simple question. The answers given were Peoria, Illinois, Kansas City, and so forth. Then one person, who insisted on sitting on the floor, said, "I came from my mother." This answer was very much in tune with Pearce's ideas.

In the United States we have for many years been ruled and regulated by the medical profession. At the moment of conception, the child's life is ordered and regulated by medical specialists. When birth is imminent, the mother is taken to the hospital, where she is placed in a sterile but drab room, laid out flat on a table with her legs up in the air, and the child is delivered abnormally. Following delivery, the child, born in a medicinal and antiseptic environment, is rushed to a medicinal and antiseptic nursery. (Although there are signs that this approach is changing, still it continues all too frequently.)

What kind of bonding occurs at this moment? The baby is bonded to the blanket in its crib, not to its mother. Linus' blanket—Linus is one of the lovable characters in Charlie Schulz's *Peanuts* cartoon—becomes the most important attachment the young child has in our somewhat sterile world of medicine. Later, in our adult life, this manifests itself as being bonded to physical possessions and abstract concepts rather than to other people. This approach to childbirth has laid a solid groundwork for all the techniques we are now rediscovering—encounter groups, self-help gimmicks, bio-feedback, Gestalt therapy, and the many others—to help us sweep out the emotional confusion in our heads. These would not be necessary if our children were brought up by nature's plan.

In the Ugandan culture of Africa, the mother works until about five minutes before the child is born. After the child is born, she puts it in a pan of warm water, not necessarily to wash it off, but rather to protect it from the shock of being born into this world. The baby is then put into a sling and carried at the mother's breast. The Ugandan baby is immediately bonded to the mother. It is held in a sling at the breast of the mother, where it can eat whenever it wants to, smile, look around, stare while the mother carries on her regular daily activities. All of the things the mother had been doing naturally while carrying the child inside, now she is doing while carrying the child outside. In some ways, this is the closest thing to the *natural* child, the state Bob Samples (1976) claims is the condition of the infant prior to birth. There is no resemblance of this birth to that in practice throughout the Western world.

Pearce emphasizes that from birth to the age of four years is the period of muscular-mindedness. All activity is of the muscular realm. We crawl on the floor with the intent of exploring the environment with every sense we have. For instance, from the window the toddler sees a mud puddle outside. All of a sudden he is able to get out the door, and he heads for that mud puddle. He oozes the warm brown stuff between his toes, his fingers, on his face. He tastes it, smells it. He tests it in any way he can with every sense. Only then Momma runs out screaming, "You bad child! You mustn't do that!" With that reprimand, a period of exploring and learning— of taking one's own chances from the beginning—is turned into a period of stress, which will manifest itself again and again as additional experiences are greeted with this same admonition.

Pearce follows that the life principle of stress and relaxation—venturing from the known to the unknown, or from safety of the self and the bonded person from others into a new experience—is basic to sound development for human beings and animals. Muscular-mindedness is developed through successful stress-relaxation practices. The maintenance of life is dependent upon the unbroken chain relationship between stress and relaxation. It all begins with that initial bond that is developed between mother and child. The child builds his muscular-mindedness on that bonding. If that bonding is incomplete, intelligence will not have a firm foundation upon which to develop.

It is adults who put fear into the child when the stress-relaxation chain is not permitted to occur, and stress-stress is substituted instead. The fear is not there initially. The child is not wrong. The child is right. This is his world. He is new to it, and he must have a safe place from which to explore it.

Jules Masserman (1966), one of music therapy's first supporters from the field of psychiatry, calls this the *Ur-defenses*. The *Ur-defenses* are the three essential but irrational faiths upon which man relies in order to quell his physical, social, and cosmic insecurities. These are: 1) the *Illusion of Personal Invulnerability, Power, and Possible Immortality*, 2) the *Hope of Brotherly Love* derived from the assumption that because one's mother loved and protected one, the rest of mankind must be almost equally supportive, and 3) a *Quest for a Celestial Order* whereby upon one's command, order can be bestowed upon a universe of chaos, in much the same way as one once was able to control one's parents.

The young child has only one idea, which is that there is no difference between himself and the universe. He cannot control the whole world, but he soon learns that his parents can do this for him. Then he learns how much control he can exert by checking out his total environment. Later he goes to school, and after school he gets a job and joins the Rotary Club, the women's movement, or a political party. We are always reaching out in some way to control the universe in our own way.

[The late] Roger W. Sperry, an eminent neurophysiologist, received a share of the 1981 Nobel Prize in medicine for his pioneering research in split-brain concepts. This "concept" (it is too early to officially label the split-brain findings as a "theory") goes further than was previously possible to explain how the nervous system functions, and how split personalities between the right and left hemispheres of the brain upset normal functioning. Sperry and his associates reached the surprising conclusion that the hemispheres have different and independent functions, that is, hemispheric specialization is normal in adult humans.

I took a proposal from Dr. Sperry for the lead-in to my doctoral dissertation. "The entire output of our thinking machine consists of nothing but patterns of motor coordination" (1952, p. 297). The young child at the age of four is experiencing this kind of motor learning. He is moving in the environment, trying to discover what it is all about. Pearce presents some evidence to support this, although he does little in the way of documentation because he is not writing from that perspective.

Before the age of four, any child with normal capabilities can be taught absolute pitch. This ability is possible because in the language development process the identifying name of an object or event becomes one of the concrete properties of that object or event. To the young child, the word and the object in the environment to which it refers are indistinguishable. If they are presented together, this will create another bonding between the child and the world, and thus an expansion beyond that tie to mother. Thus, if tonal pitches are named verbally and then produced aurally enough times before the age of four, any child with normal hearing capabilities will achieve this concept called absolute pitch.

Up to the age of fourteen, most children have available for their consideration and use almost every aspect of paranormal psychology which we adults are trying to re-discover or recover. The young child does have extrasensory perception. The young child can control sensory and physiological activity. To illustrate, Pearce relates his own experience with one of his students. A father came in one day and said, "It does work!" He recounted that his son had cut his wrist very badly and it was bleeding profusely. He took the boy on his lap, smiled, and said, "Son, we must stop the bleeding. Stop the bleeding!" The bleeding stopped. Very curious. Very interesting. The bleeding stopped because the father was bonded to the son, the son was bonded to the Earth, and the Earth and the happenings of the Earth were the same thing. For the young child, this is what it is all about. He already knows biofeedback. It is only we adults who have to wait until later in life to rediscover it. In so doing, many self-proclaimed authorities become wealthy showing us how to do what has been within our capabilities all along.

As we probe deeper, however, we discover that these paranormal abilities may be the reason junior high school adolescents are disruptive in the classroom and disconcerting to their teachers. It is conceivable that paranormal abilities are connected with the right hemisphere of the brain, and that these automatic happenings can take place before age fourteen. However, during all those years, adults have been forcing the child to conform to a restrictive, rational, practical, unimaginative world, and have inhibited the child from freely expressing these abilities. Adults have shackled his magical thinking. Pearce observed that, "Children often try to tell *us* what we in our blindness and deafness have so seriously failed to tell *them* [italics added]" (1977, p. 181). Thus, it is possible that the junior high adolescent's seemingly uncontrollable need to create a disturbance is the last gasp of the right brain in its losing battle to keep its own place in his head. Our intellectual, rational Western civilization has tried to kill right brain functioning.

The magical child before the age of fourteen years has all kinds of possibilities and potentialities. What happens to them? I have come to the conclusion that from children we receive wisdom and it takes adulthood to create babble. I can best illustrate this through poetry written by children (Pearson, 1976) describing their perceptions about their universe(s).

> Lynette, age 12
>> Dark, dark night
>> The trees. The river.
>> One more day;
>> For so slow goes the day.
>> Before the end
>>> the world goes round
>>> once more.
>> The world begins the day.
>> The night has gone.
>> The day for the end of the world
>>> once more begins.
>> Once more begins the sun
>> Slow, so slow.
>> Go on, world, live.
>> Begin, sweet sun.
>> Begin, sweet world.
>> The people live and die.
>>> people die alive
>>>> alive
>>>>> alive. (p. 6)
> Akiko, age 7
>> Mountains have nerves.
>> The roots of trees are
>> the nerves of mountains . . .
>>
>> Mountains have ears.
>> They copy what man says.
>> Everybody calls it echoes.
>> . . . echoes. (pp. 47, 50-51)

Vickie, age 13
    . . . A tree is a lady in a new
coat in spring, and nothing in
the winter because she wanted
too much . . . (p. 55)

If you think all of this about muscular mindedness is irrelevant or mystical, I have a valid explanation—Einstein's "muscle twitches" led to the equation $E=mc^2$, which, in turn, led to the atomic bomb. Einstein said that over fifty percent of his conception for the theory of relativity came from recognizing the sensory input from his own muscles. His movement within the environment generated muscular thinking. Often it was not the conscious act of intellectual thought that brought forth the solution to a technical problem. Indeed, most discoverers and creators learn that to find the solution they must forget the problem. Even at an advanced age, Einstein was still thinking with his muscles. In a manner of speaking, by twitching his index finger, Einstein discovered the atomic bomb. If this seems mystical, let it be so.

Pearce noted that the growth of intelligence relies on a sensorimotor process, a coordination of the child's muscular system with his sensory system and general brain processes. Unlike Einstein, are most of us adults too old for sensorimotor learning?

Michael Mott's poems (1976) speak to me on many levels. "And the Tree by the Water," a portion which is quoted below, seems attuned to sensory mindedness.

And the tree by the water

Excepting all who passed
and did not stop to see

how many yellow blossoms in its boughs
how many glistening branches in the winter
how many birds

——nothing was always there
. . . .

And the tree by the water

Excepting all who saw
but did not see

And the tree by the water
The tree by the water

It was not Zion we lamented

It was our exile
from our very lives   (p. 21)

This myth, as Mott labels it, seems to aptly portray our culture. In Western thought process we have tried to exile our very lives from ourselves. By that I mean that, the arts—music, dance, poetry, drama—have been shoved aside in our kneeling down and bowing to the so-called all-knowledgeable, "pure" sciences. We have tried to make the field of music academic. We have tried to make *all* fine arts academic, or "academanic"— a very appropriate adulteration. The technicalities of music as expressed through its structure, analysis, and interpretation have no meaning outside the feeling state music produces in the hearer. This is the only reality that music knows.

We are quite irrational in our approaches to certain kinds of information, believing that knowledge of the mechanics equates with understanding. As Mott says, "Excepting all who saw but did not see." We visually observe and therefore assume we see. Yet the physiological act of seeing does not produce understanding of what the eye sees, what the mind's eye, as it were, sees. We are just now only beginning to learn, however, that there is a part of the brain which is continually searching for that information to which it has been denied all too long.

Consciousness and Beyond

Author Bob Toben (1975), in a book titled *Space-time, and Beyond* claims that the "irrational" field of parapsychology is now becoming explainable by that purest of all sciences, physics. The visual style of this book is unique. The first half is presented through diagrams, charts, and even descriptive cartoons. In the second section several physical scientists of the so-called "new generation" present scientific commentary on Toben's graphical propositions. When I say "new generation," I am referring to the people whose ideas differ from those of the establishment. These gentlemen are physicists, but they operate on the leading edge of their discipline, often being too radical for acceptance by the physics community. Toben is also of this "new generation." His book is listed under the Occult in the Library of Congress cataloging system—not listed as a *Science,* but as *Occult.*

Toben's theme, offered on the basis of what scientific evidence is available now, is the possibility and even the probability that we exist in many different altered states of consciousness. We have some awareness that this is so, but we do not call it that. As an example, the reader, sitting quietly while pondering the words on these pages is in a state of consciousness that does not resemble in any way whatsoever the state of a warrior in the midst of battle. In our *normal* lives we have a representative selection of all the states of consciousness. Toben's most urgent message is that our existence in our universes is not limited to space-time, but we do not understand what is beyond. We only know there *is* a beyond.

Toben goes on to explain that we are living in a multiplicity of universes. Our identity is really the production of two cones of light, one being past experience and the other, future. The tip of each cone meets the other, assuming an hourglass configuration. The meeting of these points is our individual selves—the now. There are multiple layers of our universes. They are connected by black holes, white holes, and worm holes. Every universe resembles a piece of Swiss cheese floating on a sea of quantum foam.

We live in the quantum foam, moving in and out of an indefinite number of universes through the interconnecting wormholes. Our consciousness at any one time is merely that point in space-time signified by the junction of the two points of the cones of light. Space, time, matter, energy do not exist, yet they are existing all the time. Can we comprehend a conflict? Nothing is there. All is there. If we relate this to studies in religious training, we discover that when one finally sees the light or "the Thing"—nirvana—one sees nothing because it is all one. This is a phenomenon of beyond space-time.

Music also has this capability. Its power can transport one beyond time and space, and into a realm devoid of matter and energy. Temporality is the "stuff" which gives music its life—music is time-ordered behavior. Yet this very life-giving force is manipulatable to the extent that it can appear to be nonexistent (and perhaps it is). Thus, when the psyche of the listener is drawn totally into the music, time as a force disappears. Concurrently, space becomes meaningless except as a vessel for holding that musical sound of the music. J. T. Fraser (1975) speculates that if artistic expression derives from the artist's capacity, through his skills, to move freely among temporalities, "then music, with its intimate auditory entry into man's self-definition, is the art of arts" (p. 411). These are powerful words.

Loss of conscious or material awareness is a common experience for the performing musician who has full command of his instrument. The pianist has no tactile or muscular sensation as his fingers rip along the keyboard. The woodwind or brass player's lips appear not to exist. The singer has only the vaguest notion of how she produces that glorious sound. The listener loses contact with his physical surroundings. For a point of time while the music is playing, matter does not exist in consciousness. Because relativity theory revealed that mass is but a form of energy, the sense of energy also is lost when these material sensations disappear.

Quite simply expressed, Toben poses a very dramatic question. "Beyond space-time is everywhere—within every point of ourselves— within every point in space . . . everything is made of blackholes, so beyond time-space is not out there. It is not beyond the galaxies. It is within everything! . . . But, we don't know *what* [italics added] it is! . . . Is it pure consciousness (pp. 54, 56)? Sadly, as creatures who operate in ordinary states of consciousness, moving in multiple universes within time and space as it is created for us, we have difficulty understanding what we are, when we are, where we are.

A physicist who *does* agree with Toben is Fritjof Capra (1975), one of the few "leading edgers" of his field. He maintains that "the principal theories and models of modern physics lead to a view of the world which is internally consistent and in perfect harmony with the view of Eastern mysticism" (p. 303). In spite of these similarities of views, which could no longer be denied when man entered the atomic age, scientific attitudes have been little affected by mysticism. Most physicists today do not seem "to realize the philosophical, cultural and spiritual implications of their theories. . . . Many of them actively support a society which is still based on the mechanistic, fragmented world view, without seeing that science points beyond such a view, towards a oneness of the universe which includes not only our natural environment but also our fellow human beings" (p. 307). Einstein and Heisenberg notwithstanding, many in the physics community continue to deny that physics *includes* humans. There is so much wisdom and information to ruminate over, in Capra's words. He frequently uses the metaphors of music (sound), rhythm, or dance to explain present-day thinking in physics. In the behavioral sciences we have yet to catch up with the models after which we have patterned our science.

Man's Brains

If the brain were so simple we could understand it,
we would be so simple we couldn't!

Lyall Watson

When in the early 1960s Sperry and his associates at the California Institute of Technology made the enlightening discovery of the split-brain, it touched off a heated debate among scientists, which continues still. Not surprisingly, this discovery was considered by many purist scientists to be merely a new fad. Yet fads contain the stuff from which facts emerge. If science is honest about its claim to be searching for explanations for all the mysteries yet incomprehensible to man, then fads cannot be ignored.

More recent evidence, while not discounting the notion that man has a split-brain, indicates that the brain is capable of greater detail and complexity than a two-hemisphere system implies. Sperry's experimental subjects were post-brain surgery patients. There was no methodology for studying normal brains. Robert Ornstein (1986, Chapter 5) devised an electroencephalographic (EEG) procedure for testing thousands of persons with normal brains. Subjects were engaged in a variety of activities, such as reading stories or technical material, drawing, thinking critically or creatively (but not listening to music!). Tiny electrodes applied to the scalp emitted charges from numerous points in both hemispheres. Results revealed there to be many independent, small units of ability residing in the cerebral cortex, and more segmented and specialized centers than were known about in the later 1960s and 1970s. Thus, the brain is not simply a binary system, but a multifaceted—a multiminded one.

Also, split-brain theory now offers a better explanation than was previously available of the place the arts hold in life. To better understand this theory, it is important to understand what we already know about the brain's sensory processing system.

A cross-section view of the cerebral cortex in Figure 1 shows that the left hemisphere controls most functions of the right side of the body, while the right hemisphere controls those on the left side. There are some exceptions, such as the olfactory sense, which does not cross over. Also, most, but not all, of the hearing sense crosses over to the opposite hemisphere. The most complex exception is sight. The left field of vision in both eyes goes to the right hemisphere, while the right field of vision in both eyes is a function of the left. Hemispheric specialization, however, does not rule out the evidence that each hemisphere contains a simplified, scaled-down version of the other's dominant abilities.

Neurophysiologists over the years have led us to believe that the brain consists of a "major" and a "minor" hemisphere. From split-brain research we now understand that the right hemisphere does not hold a subdominant position or a mirror image to the misperceived "dominant" left hemisphere. Each hemisphere is major in its own areas of specialization. The intellectual, analytical, verbal, mathematical, sequential left hemisphere has been elevated in importance because it performs the functions of conventional education and training. We are made to believe only in the products of the left brain.

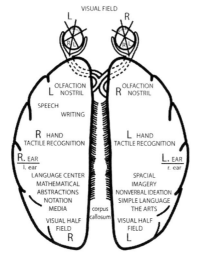

Figure 1. Lateralization of function in the two hemispheres. Adapted from Sperry (1970).

Left hemisphere functioning as we currently perceive it did not seem to exist until about 500 B.C., the period in history when the concept of chronological time—past, present, future—came into being. Mankind does not have a history before the fifth century B.C. except for what archaeologists are able to piece together and from poetry, mythology, and oral history that has been passed down from preceding generations. Prior to that time man did not conceive of history as chronological time. The relationship of past, present, and future, to a limited extent what Fraser identifies as biotemporality (1987), has been understood by mankind for only a short period of his total existence on Earth. The most complex temporality, that being the "reality of the mature human mind," Fraser labeled "nontemporality" (p. 367). In his temporal hierarchy, this is the next higher temporality above biotemporality, and is marked by a distinction among past, present, and future.

To arrive at the concept "history," man first had to understand the principle of connected events, and that these were separate from the intentions of the divinities. This required a consciousness of man's existence in time and space. With this enlightenment, history was "invented." Herodotus is credited as the father of historiography, the writing of history, in the fifth century B.C. He chronicled events in the order of their occurrence apart from the intentions of the gods (Fraser, 1975).

In tracing the breakdown of the bicameral mind, which I will cover more thoroughly later in this chapter, [the late] Julian Jaynes (1976) credits the old testament of the Bible as providing the most complete literary record. In the intervening centuries, the left hemisphere has been trained in Western cultures—although not so much in most others—to be abstract, linguistic, and numerical.

The right hemisphere, which seems to be what man worked with entirely in the time before biotemporality was understood, is concrete, intuitive, holistic, and responsible for orientation in space and artistic endeavor. It is not too far-fetched to state that left hemisphere history "stays in the words," while that in the right resides in the emotions.

Jack Fincher writes in *Human Intelligence* (1976) that nowhere is the right hemisphere in greater evidence than in the world of the artist— applying the noun to all those who engage in creative artistic endeavors— and his art.

The "state of the science" with respect to how we process musical stimuli, while not yet conclusive, does provide significant evidence about each hemisphere's role in the total process. Both hemispheres are equally able to discriminate pitches, although the left hemisphere appears better able to detect minute changes. The right hemisphere is dominant in intensity and chordal perception. Timbre, tonal memory, and melody identification also fall to the right hemisphere, as do loudness and temporality to a lesser degree. Surprisingly, no clear cerebral dominance for rhythm has yet been established; however, both hemispheres seem to be capable of rhythmic perception. Singing is a right hemisphere function. However, left hemisphere dysfunction impairs the ability to produce the lyrics though not the melody. Sequential and analytic tasks seem to be more the responsibility of the left hemisphere, while the sound field depends upon a functional right. All this by no means implies independence of the hemispheres from each other, but rather that one or the other may assume primary responsibility for a given activity. The total auditory process requires interaction between both hemispheres (Hodges, 1980).

When through education and cultural attitudes about the arts we have tried to make them academic by forcing them into a verbal-intellectual mold, we probably committed the greatest injustice possible against our humanness. The arts are a way to express or feel our differences, not our sameness. The arts should not be forced to compete on the same level with fields that demand observable behavior and testing approaches.

Robert Ornstein (1972) says that "the recognition that we possess two cerebral hemispheres which are specialized to operate in different modes may allow us to understand much about the fundamental duality of our consciousness . . . as between reason and passion, or between mind and intuition" (pp. 58–59).

These two modes of consciousness—intellectual and intuitive—complement each other. There is no major brain, no minor brain. There is nothing but two major brains, each bearing distinct and sometimes separate specialties. The complementarity concept is not new, but what is new is the physiological basis to support the long held mental and cultural understandings.

The right hemisphere has a limited vocabulary, somewhat similar to pidgin English. This vocabulary was discovered through surgery. When the corpus callosum, which is the communications network between the two hemispheres, was vastly cut, the right hemisphere was made to speak. However, if it gets too perturbed, it can produce an extensive language of profanity.

If you have a junior-high-age client who curses a great deal, you might be able to extinguish this through exposure to the holistic concepts of music, art, dance, drama, and poetry. If the client is concentrating on the arts, the right brain will not be able to curse very easily. In the process, he may discover the joys of the arts and, by cleaning up his language, acceptance from teachers and peers.

Interestingly, up to about age four, there is little difference in the hemispheres' language and speech proficiency. Through maturation, or perhaps cultural programming, the right hemisphere's ability to speak is extinguished (Gazzaniga, 1973). This idea links more than casually with the description of Pearce's "magical" child.

We must learn a whole new language—a new kind of perception about communication—much the same as was required when the new physics replaced the traditional Newtonian order. The need for a more effective language has been proclaimed by many. Physicist David Bohm (1982), whose own theories call for a new language, said, "if we can find a language in which mind and matter are seen to be of the same order, then it might be possible to discuss [the experience of immanence or transcendence of wholeness] intelligibly" (p. 207).

It is the right hemisphere that is missing from Western man's language and his perception of his world. We think subject-predicate, cause-effect, mind-matter—all linear processes, and thus of the left hemisphere. We take this logical style to the extreme by denying that communication even can occur in any other way, totally repudiating the fact that the majority of the Earth's people—Orientals, Indians, Native Americans, and Aborigines—think in a different manner. The last I heard, their brains were no different from ours, but how they use them is.

The Brain and Education

To be acceptable in Western education, the arts must subject themselves to left hemisphere scientific testing. One might believe these researchers are saying, "Yes, I know you [the arts] are here, but to convince me of your validity you must prove yourself." This attitude is doomed to failure as it always has been. We resist exposing our very personal and sometimes even sacred musical beliefs and behaviors to microscopic examination. Nor do we want the music curriculum to be predominantly an exercise in information acquisition. We want to sing, to play, to hear the music! And if we are denied this, we rebel both internally and externally. This rebellion is our right brain trying to shake off the censorship imposed by the left brain.

The right hemisphere does demand to be heard in spite of the fact that in our culture we have devalued it and attempted to shut it down. All of those fantasies, mystical ideas, and wild notions that we have are often ridiculed or discouraged. Women are given the right to be intuitive, but not men. It is women's privilege to be emotional, but men are supposed to maintain their composure under all circumstances. We construct biases and differences which are contrary to biological "laws" and make no sense whatsoever. The differences between left and right hemispheres offers the probability that the arts are necessary in the life of man and, indeed, hold the key to the explanation of the place human beings have in the universe. Erich Fromm (1968) understood this when he said, "The culture-creating group lives on the fringes. They are creative scientists and artists, but it seems that, thus far, the most beautiful blossom of the 20th century society grows on the tree of science, and not on the tree of art" (p. 33).

Is Right the Wrong Teaching Style?

For too long, learning has been perceived as a linear process made up of a continuum of lines either parallel to one another or stretched from end to end. The arts sit in their exclusive cubicle, science in theirs, religion in yet another, and so on, all isolated from one another. Granted, current educational practices have moved to the integrated studies concept, at least at the elementary level, where learning modules and satellite systems are in common vogue. However, the weakness of many integrating studies programs is the insistence that the same knowledge be stored in the same way. I prefer, instead, to think in terms of a circle of information, with relationships and sameness of all things as the hub from which specificity and discreteness radiate. That is, learning with the *whole* brain.

Our system of education centers on conformity. How do we learn to grade, judge, and recognize the growth of individuality—of newness—

growth in the sense of moving away from safety? Safety is getting an A grade. Growth may be the willingness to accept an F, and yet still retain the determination to go forward with an idea which may change the world, such as did Einstein and Edison. Now, transferring that notion to the educator, in order to succeed, teaching may have to appeal to the appropriate or best-fit image, that is, what the student believes to be true, subjective knowledge.

Educational theories tend to look only at the present, not the future. True, education does preserve and teach history, but it also *makes* it. It should furnish potentials as well as heritages. Because of this, formalism and perfect practice are impossible. Described another way, "Education," when treated as a proper noun, demands structure and control. It widens the image of what a man is not. Conversely, "education" as a common noun permits freedom and choice and widens the image of what a man is capable of becoming, and acknowledges that this can occur only by utilizing the entire brain.

Even though the split-brain dualism is still in dispute, if it is viewed as the complementary system its creators profess, perhaps a retarded or autistic child is demanding that the world stay in the right hemisphere. It is perhaps too much for some brains to be part of the mechanism that produces a larger whole or something different called the mind. Perhaps some brains would rather remain in the right hemisphere.

As I think of my own thinking process—brain, mind—I add a third dimension—the head. As best introspectively as I can feel, there is a conflict. The brain is the operator—the mechanism that provides the gestalt of the mind. But then as I try to think of my mind . . . something behind my eyes I can feel physically, something between my ears I can't quite comprehend. I can stop my breathing, I can stop my tasting, in a sense, but I can't get rid of my *feeling* for some affective gravity. Something must *touch* the base—the ground, so to speak. But I experience three dimensions, each a little greater than itself. When I say "itself," I am referring to the antiquated concept of the whole being greater than the sum of the parts. Add a neuron here, a neuron there, a neuron to the brain, and the result is the mind which thinks of something more encompassing, not greater or better, but something different than could be assumed by merely connecting one neuron to another. Then, as best I can determine, there is something called "in the head." It seems to be a little different than just the mind. Maybe that is because the Western mind is still too much a product of the rationalistic thinking of our present age of development. Too much left brain, that is.

The Arts as Healing in the Literature

For many years, I have been frustrated in my search for information about the arts and treatment for the handicapped in books that were labeled "professional education." All too often even the required texts for courses in the "exceptional children" area are woefully lacking in their coverage of the aesthetics for the handicapped. There are a number of excellent texts which focus on new ways of looking at human nature and intelligence, yet, in all probability, do not appear on reading lists for these courses. The fact that they contain major sections or even entire chapters devoted to the arts and their relation to human nature should command the attention of music therapy professors.

The nature of American education is specialization. Liberal arts, particularly the study of the great books, is all but dead. Most educational texts are written for a highly specific audience who is interested in even more highly specific subject matter. All too often this produces vacuous information devoid of any sense of relationship with the rest of the world. This is the ultimate of left hemispheric education. Yet if it is the whole person we seek to educate, authors such as Jack Fincher, Julian Jaynes, David Sudnow, J. T. Fraser, Susanne Langer, and George Leonard, to name a few, need to be acknowledged.

In a chapter titled "Athletics and Art," from *Human Intelligence,* Jack Fincher challenges the inference that athletics and the arts are not considered to be acts of intelligence. Among the many quotations he uses are a large number from musicians who speak of their beliefs about music. He goes so far as to say, "There is virtually no argument, among artists and their critics at least, that art is communication at its zenith" (p. 140). He perceives that athletics and the arts are connected because much of what we do is a knowing other than cognitive. We produce a musical sound with our bodies, knowing where to go to get that sound. This is Pearce's "muscular-mindedness." When one tries to cognize, the process is interrupted. Igor Stravinsky put it more powerfully when he said, "I haven't understood a bar of music in my life, but I have felt it" (Peter, 1977, p. 350).

One rather interesting phenomenon has been noticed when comparing the processes required of both athletes and musicians in the development of their special skills. To illustrate, when asked, "What is your memory?," the young child responds, "That's what I use to forget with." That is essentially the goal toward which the athlete and musician are aiming. They practice for the purpose of forgetting. You have to forget your muscles and the musical score in order to make that vital difference between being a musician and being a technician.

No less is required of the music therapy student in order to become a recreational instruments musician. Recreational instruments' competence is required in many college music therapy programs. Students must be able to achieve competency with such instruments as guitar, autoharp, and recorder. Not enough has been done to standardize the level of performance abilities for these instruments. One vital ability is to be able to perform well enough to establish and maintain eye contact with others. This is not possible when the therapist's head is lowered in concentration on the music or the instrument. You must be able to forget your performance on your instrument in order to relate to your clients, and, of course, relating to others is a primary requisite in therapy. That ability to establish eye contact with others should probably be specified as one of the quiz-out requirements. If applied properly, it should help produce music therapy *musicians* rather than *technicians*.

Julian Jaynes, another author not found on standard college reading lists, introduces us to bicameral man and his intertwining of music and poetry in *The Origin of Consciousness and the Breakdown of the Bicameral Mind* (1976). Jaynes is [Jaynes died November 21, 1997] not your typical psychologist, academic, or any other class of person, for that matter. He is considered a maverick, a "dilettante who ranges over many fields in which he lacks expertise," in the view of some of his colleagues. Further, his book has been described as "bold, mind-blowing, revolutionary, monomaniacal, and ridiculous" (Keen, 1977). To my mind, Jaynes' detractors may not have searched deeply enough for his meanings, which are intelligent, provocative, and poetic.

Bicameral, in Jaynes' formulation of his topic, was the state of human nature in ancient days. "At one time human nature was split in two, an executive part called a god, and a follower part called a man. Neither part was conscious" (p. 84). The absence of consciousness is incomprehensible to us. To make it comprehensible, if that is even possible, he traces poetry's roots and its reliance upon music. Ancient poetry *was* music, in a sense, for it employed a songlike cadence. When poets added the lyre or flute to their productions, it was for the purpose of transferring the excitement the music created in the right cerebral hemisphere to the left where it could be transformed into speech. Although the concept "split-brain" had no meaning, it was operating, and quite effectively, for a species which had no understanding of consciousness.

Jaynes does not allow his argument to remain in antiquity, but documents current neurological evidence supporting music as a product of the right hemisphere. In his in-depth discussion of consciousness, he once again turns to music, this time to support his argument that "consciousness is a much smaller part of our mental life than we are conscious of, because we cannot be conscious of what we are not conscious of" (p. 23) (see B.

Brown quotation, "A Re-Vision and Expansion of Processes in Music Therapy," Chapter 2).

Through example, he too asserts that the performing musician cannot be aware of the various tasks and mental processes required to perform a musical selection. There are simply too many things going on for the mind to keep in consciousness. Earlier in this chapter, I stated that the musician must relegate his muscular functioning to the unconscious if the music is to emerge.

David Sudnow is a sociologist who has written several books concerned with creativity. In *Talk's Body* (1979), he describes how he taught himself improvisatory jazz piano over a period of about six years. He sat on a stool between his piano and typewriter and improvised at whichever one appealed to him at the moment. He tells his story in flowing-through terms, rich in analogy, as the thoughts occurred to him, rather than in tightly structured prose. Improvised music-making and ordinary talking are much alike, he claims, in that both are built upon movement from place to place. "You have to get places on time," Sudnow claims. "You find places in the course of moving—without rehearsal, doing improvisation. You learn how to use your body to reach the whereabouts of places that form up the setting for such movements. . . . In both music-making and talking, there is a social world, an organization of ways of doing such movements, and an organization of ways of regarding them" (pp. 3–4).

Music as we have it is the closest thing to life that humans can express, because within it, music has combined all levels of temporalities, a psychic nature of frequency, organization into units of time, and expansion into larger forms. It must be "lived"—experienced—to exist. It is that "living experience" which provides the evidence of its existence. This is an existential concept. Most significantly, music has one dimension we cannot realize in other art forms. Music's uniqueness is that it exists on a time basis. I never cease to be startled at how smart I was when I said that "music is time-ordered behavior." I realize now that those words came from outside, not from what I had learned through formal education. Music exists in one direction, and one direction only—forward into the future. It cannot be gone backwards.

In *Of Time, Passion, and Knowledge,* Fraser (1975) talks about music and all of the arts quite extensively. He places music at the highest level, as does Schopenhauer, Goethe, Suzanne Langer, and other distinguished philosophers. Music is the "art of arts" because within the sounds of music—although not in the lyrics, which are in the left, not the right, cerebral hemisphere—all levels of temporality exist. Our musicianship is on the right side, our theory grade is on the left. Many times the "twain do not meet." The 18th century German philosopher Gotthold Lessing stated that "music is the art of time," a view that has been shared by many since then.

Within musical sounds there are different temporalities that are around us. Fraser says we do not even begin to appreciate anything above the temporal level of biological selves. In other words, we really cannot understand our humanness or beingness because we do not have the time sense for it yet. We do not understand what our "self time" is, but somehow music expresses it for us. Of all the arts, music has the closest, the most intimate attachment to biotemporality, and requires less left hemisphere information. He too is aware that music always has a future and can only be appreciated going into the future.

Editor's Summary

In this chapter, Sears sought to present an overview of the relation music enjoys with the brain, formal education, and human development. In the process, we have seen that human beings are more than mildly foolish in their attempts to struggle through this life. How little we seem to have learned through the millennia about child-rearing, the most basic and important relationship available to man. At times, it appears that civilization is moving backward—a genuine puzzlement in this supposedly highly technical, sophisticated 21st century.

A review of some of the more fascinating recent discoveries about brain function revealed that for all too long humans have been hobbled by ignoring much of the brain's abilities, particularly those located in the right hemisphere. Since many artistic capabilities appear to reside in the right hemisphere, we are left to wonder how much has been lost by such ignorance, particularly in Education's approach to learning.

So we are left to wonder about these dilemmas, and "wonder" we must if we are ever to close the gap in our knowledge between human functioning and mechanical technology.

References

Bohm, D. (1982). The physicist and the mystic—Is a dialogue between them possible? (Conversation with D. Bohm conducted by Renee Weber). In K. Wilber, *The holographic paradigm*. Boulder, CO: Shambhala.

Capra, F. (1975). *The Tao of physics*. Boulder, CO: Shambhala.

Fincher, J. (1976). *Human intelligence*. New York: G. P. Putnam's Sons.

Fraser, J. T. (1975). *Of time, passion, and knowledge*. Princeton, NJ: Princeton University Press.

Fraser, J. T. (1987). *Time, the familiar stranger*. Redmond, WA: Tempus.

Fromm, Erich. (1968). *The revolution of hope*. New York: Harper & Row.

Gazzaniga, M. S. (1973). The split brain in man. In R. E. Ornstein (Ed.) *The nature of human consciousness*. San Francisco: W. H. Freeman.

Hodges, D. A. (1980). Human hearing. In D. A. Hodges (Ed.). *Handbook of music psychology*. Lawrence, KS: National Association for Music Therapy.

Jaynes, J. (1976). *The origin of consciousness in the breakdown of the bicameral mind*. Boston: Houghton Mifflin.

Johnson, Wendell. (1965). *Verbal man: The enchantment of words*. New York: Collier Books.

Keen, S. (1977). Julian Jaynes: Portrait of the psychologist as a maverick theorizer. *Psychology Today,* November, 66–67.

Masserman, J. H. (1966). *Modern therapy of personality disorders*. Dubuque, IA: William C. Brown.

Mott, M. (1976). *Absence of unicorns, presence of lions*. Boston: Little, Brown.

Ornstein. R. E. (1972). *The psychology of consciousness*. San Francisco: W. H. Freeman.

Ornstein, R. E. (1986). *Multimind*. Boston: Houghton Mifflin.

Pearce, J. C. (1977). *The magical child*. New York: E. P. Dutton.

Pearson, J. (1976). *Begin sweet world*. Garden City, NY: Doubleday.

Peter, L. J. (1977). *Peter's quotations*. New York: Bantam Books.

Samples, B. (1976). *The metaphoric mind*. Reading, MA: Addison-Welsey.

Sperry, R. W. (1952). Neurology and the mind-brain problem. *American Scientist, 40,* 297.

Sperry, R. W. (1970). Perception in the absence of the neocortical commissures. In *Perception and its disorders. Proceedings of Association for Research in Nervous and Mental Disease*. Baltimore: Williams and Wilkins.

Sudnow, D. (1979). *Talk's body*. New York: Alfred A Knopf.

Toben, B. (1975). *Space-time and beyond*. New York: E. P. Dutton.

Wilber, K. (Ed.) (1982). *The holographic paradigm*. (Special updated issue of *Brain/Mind Bulletin*). Boulder, CO: Shambhala.

Chapter Five

The Influence of Music on Behavior

When words leave off, music begins.

Heinrich Heine (1797–1856)

In music one must think with the heart and feel with the brain.

George Szell

Editor's Introduction

A marriage of numerous ideas drawn from class lectures, conference presentations, notes, and miscellaneous other sources is the best description of what this chapter is about, with the central theme being music's influence on behavior. Much of the context was extracted from discussion between Sears and an audience, sometimes students, sometimes colleagues, but most specifically from the second of the two "Re-Vision and Expansion of the Music Therapy Processes" presentations delivered at the National Association for Music Therapy Annual conference, Dallas, TX, October 31, 1979. Chapter 2 is the first.

What Ever Happened to the Influence of Music on Behavior?

That the influence of music on behavior is basic to music therapy should produce no contradiction. Yet for some time the profession has been talking around this concept rather than facing it head on. It came about quite naturally as music therapists became knowledgeable in the various schools of psychotherapy and behavior, and incorporated the specific techniques from these schools into their practice: Music therapist and Gestalt therapy, or behavior modification, reality therapy, guided imagery, transactional analysis, and many others.

   As we immersed ourselves deeper into these schools of thought, we moved further away from the era of inquiry about the *influence of music on behavior*. I do not mean concern only about physiological responses to music, but primarily about the larger question—what is the nature and character of the influence of music on behavior? Attention was diverted away from this probing question when the psychoactive drugs were introduced into psychiatric hospitals. It became difficult to use music as a stimulant or sedative with heavily medicated patients. Then our profession expanded into other kinds of treatment institutions which advocated other kinds of treatment objectives. So music therapists became more activity oriented, and the pendulum swung to the extreme edge and away from the centeredness which can only be supplied by the music itself.

Therapist or Artist?

Yet there were other causes for neglecting the influence of music on behavior, some of which still plague the profession. One such factor is that we still have not determined what the performer role should be. We are still learning to be performers rather than therapists. The therapist needs to be a therapeutic performer, rather than the so-called artist of his instrument, and must possess sufficient artistry to convey the musical message, which is our particular reason for existing. But what does that really mean? Much more than simply acquiring the ability to chord on the guitar almost every song in the basic popular repertoire. This notion is all too widely held, the assumption often being that music therapists are deficient in musical skills and knowledge.

At the other end of the spectrum, we find the traditional approach to music learning in the typical instrumental studio. The purpose is to work with the instrument—that includes the voice, of course—long and hard enough so that the music on the printed page is consistently reproducible by the instrument. We were taught to play the music as it was written, complete with interpretive and dynamic markings that frequently were added by others long after the composer departed. Later, even more individual interpretations are incorporated by the teacher or conductor. If we have been trained in that kind of tradition, we emerge trying to imitate better and better imitations. There is nothing wrong with accomplishing something according to certain standards of perfection, but we forget what the purpose is. However, music should not be perceived as an imitative pattern only, to be drilled and performed in the same fashion as did the ancient master. We should use the ideas written down by others to relate to and incorporate into ourselves, with the purpose to produce *in* ourselves the best music (musician) therapists. Thus, it might be said that while the artist musician, by the very nature of his work, tries to make good music for people, the music therapist, by the nature of *his* work, must make music good for people.

Another academic weakness in the early days of our profession was that we frequently misapplied the abnormal psychology we learned in the classroom. We made all kinds of psychological interpretations in the clinic. For whatever reasons, we behaved as junior-grade psychiatrists. The academic support coursework is not required for the purpose of preparing one to be a professional in those fields. It is in the curriculum so that when we observe something in the clinic with our particular tool, music, we will have the knowledge and language to communicate our observations to the other specialists on the professional team.

Music Therapy Symbolization System

A second factor which has contributed to a somewhat torpid attitude toward the influence of music on behavior is the absence of a music therapy symbolization system. However, in my judgment, constructing a symbolization system in music therapy is more complicated than in many other fields because music is temporal as opposed to spatial. Music exists only in time; thus, a model consisting of visual symbolizations, which are spatial, creates an additional separation between the entity itself and its cognitive expression. That is to say, to explain a temporal entity, one must first transform it into a spatial system—words—which in turn must be transformed into a cognition system—the brain. In this thought we can find similarities to split-brain theory, which perceives the right hemisphere as vertical or nonlinear, while the left hemisphere is horizontal or linear. Put the two operations together and you have both dimensions creating reality. Is the combination of left and right brain the proper way—maybe the *only* way—to construct a music therapy symbolization system?

In physics theory, if an object accelerates fast enough, the two lines which are on axes tend to merge into one, and both time and energy are the same thing. Everything disappears back to the original set, as far as I can understand physics these days.

Einstein's special theory of relativity showed that to the stationary observer, a moving object appears to contract in its direction of motion and to become shorter as its velocity increases, until, at the speed of light, it disappears altogether. However, this effect is not experienced by the observer who is traveling *with* the object. To him, the stationary observer is moving and he is at rest. Einstein applied the terms "proper" and "relative" to these phenomena. "Proper" always appears to be normal and applies to observer and object moving together in harmony, whereas the condition is "relative" when observer and that being observed are in different frames of reference (Zukav, 1979).

Quite appropriate to this is a concept expressed in Chapter 6 of the present work, "Time, the Servant of Music:" "In the behavioral sciences, the moment we impede on another person's environment, we are moving that person out of the way. What we thought we could accomplish with him . . . at the time we started changes because the person has also moved away from the point at which he . . . started." I perceive this to be the meaning of

Einstein's special theory of relativity as applied to human beings. We have a hard job. People are the hardest "objects" to study.

Yes, this medium we have needs no words. "As soon as one is impelled to speak about [music], all the concepts usually employed in life go to pieces," claims Rudolf Steiner (1970). "It is scarcely possible to speak about music in terms customarily used in ordinary life. This is simply because music does not exist in the physical world given to us. It must first be brought into being in this given physical world" (p. 113). Yet this may be the paramount reason it is so difficult to justify our existence to the regulators, those persons who administer the treatment facilities, and thus determine who will provide therapy for their patients/clients. Of course, we can demonstrate music's value. Unfortunately, the regulators then erroneously interpret that it is recreation, and thus should come under the aegis of Recreation Therapy.

This misunderstanding, to a large extent due to the absence of a viable symbolization system, confuses us. Our response is to substitute *what* we do as being more important, in a sense, than *why we do it*. By analogy, we worry more about the technique of reaching out our hand than just putting the hand out to be grabbed. We go to workshops because we need them, but we misunderstand what that need is. We tend to go to those that espouse a point of view with which we already agree. We tend not to go to those events which approach the subject from a different direction and with which we do not agree. We tend to read what we agree with; we tend to listen to what we agree with. We do not even try to explain it to ourselves, let alone attempt to examine the deeper meaning of our attitudes. All of these acts tend to separate us from our primary raison d'être—the influence of music on behavior.

E. Thayer Gaston (1966) attempted to demonstrate this phenomenon at an American Psychiatric Association conference. His verbal presentation was very brief, for the message was constructed around live musical performances. Gaston explained to the audience that the purpose of the demonstration was to allow each listener to determine for himself the effects of the musical selections as each was performed.

When the national anthem was played, the entire audience promptly rose to its feet. By this example, Gaston demonstrated not only that a musical message did not need words to be understood but also the effect of conditioning. The potency of the message lay in the affective response each listener experienced, which could not be demonstrated through the spoken word. We could demonstrate it, and all the psychiatrists, in a sense, nodded their heads in understanding.

Gaston (1955) lectured elsewhere and often on music's influence, asserting its primacy not only as a therapeutic precept, but as an "everyday occurrence [in all peoples' lives, although] we often fail to take notice of it"

(p. 154). One simply could not come within his orbit without committing to music's influence in one fashion or another. "Music is an essential and necessary function of man," he maintained. "It influences his behavior and condition[,] and has done so for thousands of years" (1968, p. 15). Simply put, man's humanness stems in large measure from his music. It matters not how primitive or sophisticated his culture is, music "brings changes and responses" (1952, p. 60).

He believed this power could be well demonstrated through functional music, that is, music performed for specific, useful purposes prescribed by the culture to which it is attached, rather than music explicitly executed for one's listening pleasure—"music for music's sake," that is. Persons of authority realized that in order to be effective and commanding leaders, their rituals needed persuasion by some powerful force. So, music was performed, and the people responded. But it is a two-way street, Gaston (1968) reminded us—"Music is shaped by culture[,] but in turn influences that culture of which it is a part" (p. 21).

Perhaps the leaders of these ancient cultures also recognized the importance of music as nonverbal communication, which was non-threatening and therefore a viable tool for molding desired behavior. Even in some present-day cultures, one is not permitted to hear certain music, or even see the instruments used to play it, unless it is the right time of the year, or the time for a specific ritual, or the time to hold a certain festival. Societies that elaborate rhythm tend to be percussive in behavior, while those that elaborate melody and harmony tend to keep a fairly constant social structure. Yet much earlier in man's evolution by the reckoning of some scholars, including Rudolf Dreikurs (1954), there is strong evidence that music preceded language in man's evolution. In support of this, we know that very early in our lives, before language development occurs, the infant learns to sing. His cooing is a primitive form of singing. Linguistic studies indicate that this same sequence holds true in all cultures, but music is so much a part of us that we fail to recognize its power to overcome the limitations of language which serve more to separate than to unite us.

Music therapists of today primarily use functional music. Much of it we know as folk or popular music. Functional music also includes musical training systems such as Orff and Kodaly. Of course, Gaston (1952) stressed what all music therapists know, and that is that to influence "appropriate" behavior, the "proper" application of music is required. "Appropriate" and "proper" are perplexing words unless accompanied by definition and explanation. This—definition and explanation—is exactly what is demanded in order to unlock the secrets shrouding the nature of music's power to influence behavior, and that mechanism exists whereby "music and its influences can be studied scientifically" (1968, p. 27), that being behavioral science methodology. Accordingly then, it is imperative to raise the question, "What ever happened to the influence of music on behavior?," notwithstanding my earlier disclaimers.

Responding to Music

Yet we rise from our chairs (as Gaston demonstrated with the doctors) when stimulated by music other than the national anthem, and for different reasons. For example, the scale ascends, the volume increases, and one rises up. This effect is well demonstrated at rock music concerts through excessive amplification. The amplified bass tones course through the entire body and the response is total. The loudest applause is generated by stimulative music, not because stimulative music is better or more enjoyable, but because of the enhanced energy it generates (Gaston, 1952). The performer is allowing us to respond in any way we choose, and possibly beyond permissible limits. By way of contrast, why is it that when played gently within the audible loudness range, bass tones tend to let us sit back and relax? There is some thought that the reason rock music is played at such a high decibel loudness level, besides forcing it to the head harder and thus overdoing it because of a deficit of right brain food, so to speak, is that they are actually trying to force the music into the feeling rather than the hearing sense. The effect is that the music actually shakes the body. Of course, it has to be very loud for that to happen because we are made of pretty elastic tissue. We will flex a bit in response to bass tones, but much less so to those at the higher registers. This is the influence of music on behavior.

It seems to me rather interesting that the tones we use for rhythm, which are usually in the bass register, are of the same frequencies that show to be the best frequencies for physical massage. One of these days, instead of the old steam bath, you may be able to walk into a little cabinet that encloses you up to the neck, get all hooked up—"wired for sound"—and then turn on the machine. You will have the volume control knob and can turn it up to whatever loudness level you can tolerate.

During our college days, we were required to read all of those studies that reported on physiological responses such as these. How frequently do we incorporate their findings in our work? More importantly, how many of us have made any effort to heed Gaston's call to further validate or refute these through our own scholarly research?

In a similar vein, an article appeared some time ago in the *Music Educators Journal* titled "An Autochthonous Approach to Music Appreciation" (Taylor, 1949). That is an awfully imposing title for the simple little notion that an appreciation for music is natural. The author, a first grade teacher, was reluctant to teach music to her pupils. She liked classical music, but felt she just did not know enough to teach others. So, she did not have music in the classroom. Most of her pupils were migrant children. They were often hyperactive, and exhibited poor concentration abilities. More by accident than design, one day during a morning milk break, the teacher played a recording she enjoyed. The normally noisy period was transformed into naptime for some of the children. She later began playing music during the lunch hour. Although the steady chatter did not stop, the tension that she had previously observed diminished. Occasionally, as the music was playing, a pupil might ask who wrote it or whatever other information he was curious about. The teacher never went any further than to give the shortest answer possible. In an unobtrusive manner, she gradually incorporated music into the regular studies and discovered that the children seemed to enjoy the so-called "good" music. Without words she was saying, "Here it is," and the children responded by developing a rather sophisticated understanding and appreciation of music, because, as the article title stated, it was natural to do so.

"Gloomy Sunday" was a popular Hungarian tune written by Rezsoe Seres in 1933. Paul Robeson introduced the English version to the United States in 1936. It was banned by the Hungarian government on the claim that it had been responsible for an outbreak of suicides. Although the U.S. government did not take such drastic measures, some radio stations and nightclubs imposed their own censorship.

Music has also been used as an aid to defeat armies. The tune "Lili Marlene" comes to mind. It was originally written by the Germans as propaganda to breed discontent and desertion within the allied forces during World War II. The words were intended to depress the warrior who was far from home. However, the actual response was grossly different from what was intended. The melody created greater emotional affect than did the words, and the song became an instantly popular marching song as the troops went into battle in the North African campaign. The Australian song "Waltzing Matilda" possesses a unique quality capable of evoking a variety of patriotic emotions, although the words, when translated from the idiomatic to English, belie any apparent patriotism.

Power of the Octave

What is this mysterious power of music? Steiner, an Austrian psychic whose training was in philosophy and science, dedicated his life to establishing a "spiritual science"—the synthesizing of science and religion—in the accepted scientific meaning. He gained and continues to enjoy the respect of great thinkers worldwide, notwithstanding his occultist practice. Not the least of his achievements were the founding of the

Waldorf School movement and learning clinics for the retarded called Campbell Villages.

Most significant to us in the music "business," Steiner (1998) held that the arts are "crucial for translating 'spiritual science' into social and cultural innovation" (paragraph 6). Some of his ideas may be troubling to the person who strives to understand music on scientific, objective, and logical levels, yet a deeper examination of his writings reveals that his awe of music is akin to our own. Listen to his words: "Now[,] it is the peculiarity of music that it should neither ascend completely into the realm of ideas [head], nor . . . descend entirely into the realm of the will [heart]," (1970, p. 136). At the same time, using three musical elements by example, he perceives that harmony tends to want to be experienced in the heart, melody in the head, and rhythm in the limbs. Does this have a familiar ring? It should, for five decades later the world would be introduced to the split-brain theory. Steiner was ahead of his time.

In his book titled *Art in the Light of Mystery Wisdom*, Steiner states that in ancient days music with sounds separated by less than an octave was incomprehensible. That is, it was not possible to produce harmonies utilizing intervals smaller than an octave. Later, although still quite ancient, the experience of the interval of the fifth was accepted.

The feeling for the third is more recent. Accepting the interval of the third produced a major musical breakthrough because it introduced the concept of major and minor, and recognized the differences between these two moods. When man was able to comprehend the feelings for major and minor, the subjective element became a complete experience, not just transitory as with the fifth, and he began to link music with his feelings of the destiny of ordinary life. "Now the connection between music and the subjective aspects of the soul begins to appear. So now man can give different shades of colour to his music. Sometimes he is within himself, sometimes outside; the soul swings back and forth between self-surrender and self-containment" (Steiner, 1970, p. 121). Whether operating at the external or internal level, the power of the musical experience is its involvement with the whole human being.

One of these days, Steiner (1970) predicts, "when man has achieved a still stronger degree of inwardness, he will have a feeling for the second and then finally for the single tone" (p. 143). Expanding further on the concept of the single musical tone, "when the inner wealth of feeling experienced in melody is transferred to the single tone, when man discovers the secret of the single tone, in other words when man not only experiences intervals but is also able to experience with inner richness and variety the single tone as if it were a melody [the ultimate experience will have been achieved.] This is something which today can be scarcely imagined" (p. 168).

The feeling we experience for the octave is indistinguishable from the tonic, which is not the true feeling. Pythagoras explained the laws of "proportions" in music whereby changing the length of a vibrating body affects the musical pitch. He determined that the octave is the most important relationship in music, followed by the intervals of the perfect fifth and perfect fourth. These continue to remain to this day the three fundamental intervals upon which music is constructed. Steiner (1970) further predicts that at some future time the octave will be experienced quite differently and distinct from the tonic. Then musical experience will be deepened and "whenever an octave asserts itself in a musical work of art, man will indeed have a feeling . . . [of having] 'found my ego anew [the physical inner ego—tonic—and the spiritual outer ego—octave—], as a human being I am exalted through the experience of the octave'" (p. 115). This revelation (or is it evolution?) will offer the proof for mankind, Steiner asserts, that God does exist.

Two other theories that assess the importance of the octave are noteworthy. Portnoy (1963) judged that "the interval of the octave is a natural phenomenon; [whereas] the tempered intervals within the octave are manmade" (p. 78).

In discussing the motion of tones, Zuckerkandl (1956) said:

> We go toward a tone by going away from it. The distance in pitch from the point of departure increases with every step, but with the eighth tone we are again at the point of departure. Leaving has become returning; start has become goal.
>
> This is the phenomenon that has fittingly been called "the miracle of the octave"; Ernst Kurth characterizes it as "one of the greatest riddles . . . the beginning of irrationality in music, a thing unparalleled in all the rest of the phenomenal world."
>
> . . . The eighth tone [of the scale] is not simply the higher repetition of the first[,] but the attained goal. . . . The phenomenon of the octave reveals the structure of the world of tone. . . . Formulations that in the world of space are paradox, indeed nonsense—wherever we go, we return; start and goal are one and the same; all paths travel back to their own beginnings—are in the world of tone, simple statements of fact. (pp. 102–104)

Another view implying the comfort found in the octave comes from Juan Roederer (1982), a physicist, space-scientist, and organist with a strong curiosity about the relation between music and physics. He claims that "the octave is the only interval (besides unison) whose component tones, when sounded together or in succession, do not introduce new resonance regions in activation pattern of the basilar membrane, since the harmonics of the upper tone coincide with the even harmonics of the lower tone. Therefore, a certain signal of similarity of identity is evoked—that pertaining to all notes different by one or more octaves" (p. 41).

Pythagoras, Portnoy, Roederer, Steiner, Zuckerkandl, and so many others appear almost mystified by the power of the octave and the influence it exerts on behavior. The octave, thus, signifies home, security, safety, comfort, all those feelings which positively bear upon behavior. If they are correct, music's influence extends beyond a complete thought or theme to a single note. Indeed, it is possible that we live in a universe of "musics" rather than music, and by extension, that we have musics therapy, and that we may soon need to consider separating the different specialties within it because the word is too big for comprehension by any of us.

What Makes Music?

What makes music—in an analytic sense, that is? The answer—music! It is not reducible. There is no whole which can be reduced from the sum of its parts without the result being nothing more than individual, disparate notes. This is not the same as Gestalt psychology, which states that the whole is greater than the sum of its parts. Music starts in the reverse direction. No musical event can be ascertained as truly made up of the sum of the parts below—the micro—or the sum of the parts above—the macro. Music is music, each work a complete expression, incapable of being anything but what it is—a perfect, unbroken thought.

Why has music, and those who produce music in all its variants, been considered a "frill" in our educational system and our culture in general? Possibly, because music is an art, its tangible value is in question. However, music is recognized to be among the most, if not the most presentable, the most personal of all communications media, rather than simply an art for art's sake. Music is people-to-people communication. The celebrated 19th century philosopher Arthur Schopenhauer (1950) put it better than I when he said, "[music is not like other arts; it is not] the copy of the Ideas, but the *copy of the will itself*, whose objectivity the Ideas are. This is why the effect of music is so much more powerful and penetrating than that of the other arts, for they speak only of shadows but it speaks of the thing itself" (p. 333). Do not ever forget his words.

Music therapy is "the copy of the will itself," a "living" therapy, meaning that every time we meet our patients we are engaging in a process of the present moment. Therefore, we must select a dynamic symbolization orientation. This orientation, to the best of my knowledge, is only that which is based upon behavior, and thus the influence music exerts on the person. Maybe the true greatness of us in the music business is not determined by the analysis of what we do, but how long succeeding generations will try to interpret it.

Hearing—King of the Senses

Perhaps the strongest case that can be made for the importance of the influence of music on behavior is the pervasiveness of the sense of sound. It is not possible physiologically to totally block out sound and, therefore, music. Think about that for a moment. It is most profound that sound is the only major sense that man, and animals so far as I know, cannot willfully— or voluntarily—shut down. This relates more than casually to Schopenhauer's "copy of the will itself." A sense organ that cannot voluntarily be shut down nor cut off must be capable of producing reality, not mere shadows. This profundity has been expressed by many scholars, but, for me, no one stated it better than [the late] Julian Jaynes (1976) when he wrote, "Sound is a very special modality. . . . We cannot turn our back on it. We can close our eyes, hold our noses, withdraw from touch, refuse to taste. We cannot close our ears though we can partly muffle them. Sound is the least controllable of all sense modalities. . . ." (pp. 96–97). And organized sound is music. Lacking the ability—actually, the power—to control the aural senses, does it not follow that the sounds that impact the hearing mechanism exert a strong influence on man's behavior?

Literature Search

What can be found in the literature of the field that supports the centrality of the influence of music in the music therapy profession? A thorough examination is beyond the scope of this paper, but a search of the title "Influence of Music on Behavior" certainly seemed worthy and manageable. *Music Therapy Index* (Eagle, 1976) seemed the logical starting point. Of the three volumes printed, between 1976 and 1980, only Volume I contained any citations with "influence of music" in the title. There are six, none of which also included "on behavior." Not even the seminal work *Music in Therapy* (Gaston, 1968) bears such a title, although the Index lists two articles containing the subject "music: effects on behavior" (Sears, 1968; Howery, 1968). Granted, the absence of the specific title does not verify that the topic is not covered in the literature; however, it does point to the directions taken by the authors. Many years ago, Diserens and Fine (1939) went so far as to title their book *A Psychology of Music: The Influence of Music on Behavior.*

So why do we shy away from the referent that identifies our profession more than any other? Why do we not attend more vigorously or address by name in scholarly papers that which gives music its power? Of course, "influence" is occurring whether or not we are mindful of it. Yet how can we be true to our profession, or more to the point, how can we be legitimate music therapists, unless we directly and consciously attend to our roots?

The explanations set forth herein, no matter how compelling, do not "explain." They merely *describe* a world viewpoint at the moment in time from which a conclusion was reached, stated first, and then explained later. We are faced with a kind of circular motion. Nonetheless, the "description" of why the influence of music on behavior has lost its appeal is strong enough to cause us to pause. Most importantly, it should persuade—no, demand—that we search for the facts. Where do we find the facts? The *nonverbal world of reality* is the world of "facts." It is the world of the senses—sight, sound, touch, taste, smell. "Statements of fact" can never *be* facts because these are verbal. Thus, only through observations of the senses (primarily aural) can we make a statement of fact that music influences behavior.

It is no longer acceptable for us to rationalize away the search for facts to support music's influence. If we are true to our belief that music therapy is a bona fide, undisputed treatment medium, then we will promptly set about to answer the question, "What ever happened to the influence of music on behavior?"

Editor's Summary

This chapter sought to answer the question, "What ever happened to the influence of music on behavior?" The introduction of psychoactive drugs contributed to this conundrum, as did the music therapy profession's confusion over what the nature of the therapist's musical abilities should be.

There is no written system for the music therapy discipline, which is compounded by the difficulty of creating a model for a field which is temporal rather than spatial. It is easier to relate to a system one can see, touch, or smell, for example, rather than one that flows through space. Searching back into music's beginnings, evidence reveals that functional music preceded art, or aesthetic, music. Whether part of primitive or sophisticated societies, humans freely respond to music. In some minds, music preceded language.

The power of music is illustrated by the octave, which many scholars, specifically Rudolf Steiner, believe is worthy of special attention. Sears claimed that music is the most presentable, the most personal of the communicative arts. It is not reducible to its individual parts. This is not well understood even by educators and scholars, in general, who often consider music a frill. How surprising that is about a stimulus whose organic sense—sound—is the most potent and invasive in man's sensory arsenal.

The music therapy literature[1] scarcely addresses the influence of music by name. If the discipline is ever to receive general recognition, this must change by developing a sound body of research, and intentionally examining why music influences behavior.

References

Diserens, C. & Fine, H. (1939). *A psychology of music: The influence of music on behavior*. Cincinnati: College of Music.

Dreikurs, R. (1954). The dynamics of music therapy. In M. Bing (Ed.), *Music therapy 1953: 3rd book of proceedings of the National Association for Music Therapy* (Vol. 3). Lawrence, KS: National Association for Music Therapy.

Eagle, C. T. (Ed.). (1976). *Music therapy index* (Vol. I). Lawrence, KS: National Association for Music Therapy.

Gaston, E. T. (1952). The influence of music on behavior. *University of Kansas Bulletin of Education, 6*, 60.

Gaston, E. T. (1955). Nature and principles of music therapy. In E. T. Gaston (Ed.), *Music therapy 1954: 4th book of proceedings of the National Association for Music Therapy* (Vol. 4). Lawrence, KS: National Association for Music Therapy.

Gaston, E. T. (1966). Sound and symbol. *Journal of Music Therapy, 3*(3), 90–92.

---

[1] Over twenty years have passed since the above chapter was written, and thus one must ask what has occurred in the intervening years. A review of the official publications of the National Association for Music therapy and its successor organization, the American Music Therapy Association, the *Journal of Music Therapy* and *Music Therapy Perspectives*, for articles bearing "influence of music on behavior" somewhere in the title was conducted for the years 1990-2005. It was felt that this size collection of the literature constituted a somewhat reliable sampling. Only one article (Silber, 1999) contained the phrase, albeit a variation, in the title. However, when "effect" was substituted for "influence," numerous titles were identified, although in no case did the specific phrase appear as it is employed in this article, i.e., "the 'effect' of music on behavior."

The Editor is not assuming that these words were inaccurately treated as synonyms by the respective authors, rather to take note that there is a relational definition factor between the two. If each use of the word "effect" found in the sampling is correct by Webster's dictionary, then we must assume that there has not been a resurgency of this agonizing question let alone any legitimate effort to face it head on.

Gaston, E. T. (1968). Man and music. In E. T. Gaston (Ed.), *Music in therapy*. New York: Macmillan.

Howery, B. I. (1968). Music therapy for the severely retarded. In E. T. Gaston (Ed.), *Music in therapy*. New York: Macmillan.

Jaynes, J. (1976). *The origin of consciousness and the breakdown of the bicameral mind*. Boston: Houghton Mifflin.

Portnoy, J. (1963). *Music in the life of man*. New York: Holt, Rinehart and Winston.

Roederer, J. G. (1982). Physical and neuropsychological foundations of music: The basic questions. In M. Clynes (Ed.), *Music, mind, and brain*. New York: Plenum Press.

Schopenhauer, A. *The world as will and idea*. (Vol. I). (R. B. Haldane and J. Kemp, Trans.). New York: Charles Scribner's Sons. (Original work published 1818).

Sears, W. W. (1968). Processes in music therapy. In E. T. Gaston (Ed.), *Music in Therapy*. New York: Macmillan.

Silber, F. (1999). The influence of background music in the performance of the Mini Mental State Examination with patients diagnosed with Alzheimer's disease. *Journal of Music Therapy, 36*(3), 196–206.

Steiner Books Anthroposophic Press. (1998). About Rudolf Steiner (paragraph 6). In *Rudolf Steiner*. Retrieved August 26, 2005, from http://www.steinerbooks.org/aboutrudolf.html

Steiner, R. (1970). *Art in the light of mystery wisdom*. (Johanna Collis, Trans.). London: Rudolf Steiner Press. (Original work published 1935).

Taylor, K. S. (1949). An autochthonous approach to music appreciation. *Music Educators Journal*, *35*(4), 17–19.

Zuckerkandl, V. (1956). *Sound and symbol*. Princeton, NJ: Princeton University Press.

Zukav, G. (1979). *The dancing Wu Li masters*. New York: William Morrow.

Chapter Six

Time, the Servant of Music

Time doesn't seem to pass here [in Rivendell]:
it just is.

J. R. R. Tolkein, *Lord of the Rings*

Time is the indestructible quality that exists
throughout eternity. . . . To waste time is to waste
your life away, for this unrecapturable quality has
no resale use. It cannot be reused, because it
never backs up or retreats.

Ruth Montgomery's spirit guides,
A Search for the Truth

Editor's Introduction

The subtext of this work is "Time," as has been borne out frequently, one chapter after another. It was apparent in the course of organizing Sears' thoughts that "Time" was always at the forefront of his thinking. Simply leaving his concepts sprinkled throughout the various chapters did not give the topic the prominence warranted. Thus, I have pulled passages which focus on "Time" from the aggregate, except where specific references needed to be retained in their original locations. These are found in other chapters.

Linking together statements from disparate sources to create a homogeneous, coherent leitmotiv was challenging, although in time logic broke through, an organizational thread was discovered, and pieces of the puzzle began to fall into their proper places. The following chapter is the result of that effort.

Very early in the process the title emerged. Unfortunately, I did not know if the premise was accurate. Yes, I had acquired knowledge and experience over time that confirmed for me that time is music's servant. Equally important, my "gut" feeling convinced me. But was that enough? I think I need go no further than to quote from the late David Epstein: "More than any other musical dimension, time depends on forces *outside its own proper domain* [italics added]—that is, time depends upon sound" (1981, p. 184).

What's to Come

Music demands time-ordered behavior. It exists only through time, requiring the individual to commit himself to the experience moment by moment. This is music's uniqueness. Upon this concept, Chapter 2 in Gaston's *Music in Therapy* (1968) was built. An argument was made that may or may not have been compelling to the individual reader of that work. It was far from exhaustive. A number of powerful statements were made which most music therapists could support on the basis of their experience, yet these statements were neither amplified nor verified. A stronger case needs to be made and will be attempted here, although no claim is made that it will be exhaustive either, for that is beyond the scope of the present work, as it was in the earlier one.

"Music is time-ordered behavior' is a quite profound statement, replete with many questions, some which are, as yet, unanswerable. Not the least of these is, "What is time?" In spite of the volumes that have been written on this exceedingly compelling theme, man still cannot pin down the meaning of time. (It is curious that as yet no universally acceptable term for the study of time has been established.) Yet the search for an answer continues, and it is this search which must be undertaken if any understanding is to be brought to the concept "music is time-ordered behavior."

The topic will be approached from three perspectives. First, we will look at a number of ideas about time from the pens of some highly regarded scholars. This discussion will center, of course, on man's perceptions and even misperceptions about time. From there the discussion leads directly into temporal distortions in mental illness. Finally, the temporality of music will be explored.

King Richard II, in Shakespeare's so-titled play, soliloquizes shortly before his untimely death,

> Music do I hear?
> Ha, ha! Keep time. How sour sweet music is
> When time is broke and no proportion kept!
> So it is in the music of men's lives.

In the course of our present journey, we hope to learn why music goes sour "when time is broke."

Time—Fusion and Confusion

Time is associated with rhythm and change, speed and velocity, social behavior, duration and sequence, yet is none of these. For eons, "What is time?" has been the great question of philosophy and religion. It is something outside us over which we have no control, something that appears absolute, yet it is also internal and eternal. We are influenced by earlier ideas, prejudices. What is commonly perceived as time is based on false prejudice. Experiences in time are diverse. There is more than one concept of time—so many, in fact, that man cannot claim to know them all, let alone what they measure or describe. There is the time of the philosopher, the psychologist, the physicist, the poet, the biologist, the clock, the sundial, the calendar, the sun and all the heavenly bodies, and even the time to boil rice.

Alvin Toffler and Frederick Melges have defined time in two interesting and contrasted ways. "Two situations alike in all other respects," Toffler (1970) says, "are not the same at all if one lasts longer than another" (p. 32). More erudite, but no more revealing, Melges (1982) claims, "In its broadest sense, time can be considered as a construct that refers to the perception or imputation of changes against some background that is taken to be relatively permanent" (p. 7).

J. T. Fraser, the pre-eminent *time* scholar, has spent his entire life attempting to unravel the secrets of *time*. His considerable knowledge notwithstanding, he admits that "seeking a comprehensive view of time is a task comparable to putting together a jigsaw puzzle whose pieces are alive and moving" (1975, p. 5). What a colorful metaphor! Admitting that a comprehensive view is not what we are after (nor does this author possess Fraser's knowledge of the subject), nonetheless, focusing on some of the more salient features of time should lead us to a better understanding of music as time-ordered behavior.

In *Of Time, Passion, and Knowledge*, Fraser (1975) states that time is generally perceived as a single, understandable, and recognizable feature of the world, when, in fact, it is instead "a hierarchy of distinct temporalities corresponding to certain semiautonomous integrative levels of nature" (p. 435). This idea confounds us, and we do not understand its implications. Incidentally, the Melges' definition of time quoted above is attributed to Fraser.

Simply stated, Fraser identifies five such temporalities or temporal states. The most primitive and strange he calls *atemporal*, this being the time of light—the world of electromagnetic radiation. The next level up in the hierarchy is the world of elementary particles, *prototemporality*, which is characterized by undirected, non-flowing, non-continuous events for which precise location is meaningless.

The simplest form of continuous time is *eotemporality*, the reality we know as the astronomical universe of massive matter. *Biotemporality* encompasses all living organisms. The concepts of past, present, and future, though limited, are introduced at this level. The ultimate level we can speak about at this stage of identification is *nootemporality,* or noetic time, the time of the human mind. This is the time which is signified by man's long-term memory.

Yet we are aware of the lesions of time (or better put, time*s*), and acknowledge that variations exist in our perception of the speed of time. The time that is expressed on the clock, which is regular and predictable, is *knowledge time,* or *time understood,* in Fraser's terminology. Put another way, it is one "thing" after another.

Quite a different experience is inner time—that time we feel within—which Fraser calls *passion* or *felt time. Passion time* is the feeling that time is either fast or slow based upon our experiences within a given time frame, which can be characterized when we say, "Gee, that was a long hour," or "Is it already 3 o'clock?" It happens as we listen to music also. Conscious attention to the passage of time can influence the perceived duration of a composition, estimating it to be longer than when not attending specifically to time. Kramer (1988) noted yet another musical example of this "time-order error" in the "tendency to perceive the first of two durational spans as either longer or shorter than the second simply because it was experienced first" (p. 332).

Human behavior scholars identify this as psychological or the inner time of the mind. It is not simply a perception by the mind, but rather a significant component of self-awareness. Einstein said it best. "When a man sits with a pretty girl for an hour, it seems like a minute. But, let him sit on a hot stove for a minute—and it's longer than an hour. That's relativity" (Barwick, 1970, p. 38). *Felt time* is relative. It is found in the flow of our consciousness. More precisely, it *is* consciousness—thinking, if you will.

Toffler (1970) says that man's temporal perceptions are linked to his internal rhythms, whereas his responses to time are culturally conditioned. Also important to the understanding of psychological time is Sam Keen's claim that the inner time sense records intensity and importance of experience rather than duration (Keen & Fox, 1973). Keen, like Einstein and Kramer, infers that "duration" is a slippery element which refuses to stay put. Thus, it appears judicious that we leave it in the hands of our imagination and memory.

Fraser (1975) systematically explains his theory of time as a conflict, with the principal combatants being *knowledge time* and *passion time*. Conflict is necessary to all systems—micro and macro—and thus it is inappropriate to think of conflict in the negative sense. In living systems the conflict/stress is between growth and decay. Yet it is unresolvable and necessary to the life of the form. Life lasts only so long as the conflict lasts. In reference to the mind, "this struggle may sometimes be described as that between knowledge felt and knowledge understood [between passion and knowledge] . . . knowledge untamed by passion is dangerous, while passion uninformed by knowledge is useless" (p. 444). Marie-Louise von Franz (1978) prefers Nicholas Cusanus' definition of time, that being "a coincidence of opposites" (p. 29). "A coincidence of opposites." I like that. Cusanus, also known as Nicholas of Cusa, was a well regarded 15th century (1401–64) German philosopher, scientist, and Catholic cardinal whose concepts continue to attract attention (Alexander, 1956, p. 604).

We understand conflict as a necessary symbiotic state in most systems, so why should it not exist in time as well? The multiplicity of temporalities, or time bases, while conflict-laden allows the continuation of all systems, humans included. There are "times" in our dreams. There are "times" in our altered states of consciousness. There are "times" which to us appear to be simultaneous or instantaneous. There are "times" which appear to us as infinity. But every kind of situation—everything we know about—has its own time scale. A "hierarchy of distinct temporalities" may not be so difficult to fathom after all, and its absence may produce boredom, which to Keen is imprisonment in one time zone.

Knowledge time may be more recognizable as linear or *monochronic* time, a concept associated with Western man specifically but not, by any means, mankind in general. To bring this thought into even sharper focus, linear time is of relatively recent origin. The ancients believed time to be cyclical—heroes repeating themselves. Not until about 500 B.C. did historians start writing in chronological historical time. Fraser (1987) would push back that date to the ninth century B.C., and credit an unnamed Yawist writer who set down the history of Israel, although not in exact chronological order, from which the Old Testament of the Bible emerged.

Herodotus (c.484–c.429 B.C.) (1972), proclaimed as the "father of history," wrote, "here set down to preserve the memory of the past by putting on record the astonishing achievements both of our own and of other peoples . . ." (p. 1). This writing style would not be possible without a linear or *monochronic* sense of time. As recent as is linear time in man's history, the mechanical clock—the most exact time measuring device we know of to date—is a mere babe, having been invented by Galileo as recently as 1642.

Monochronic time is linear, segmented, sequential, and spoken of in tangible terms, such as "saved," "spent," "wasted," "lost," "made up," "expired," and "handled." We are inclined to view *monochronic* time sense as if it were built into the universe rather than a learned, imposed, and arbitrary perception. True, it is an efficient method of handling time, but not necessarily the only useful way. Some cultures are *polychronic,* that is, cyclical or nonlinear. Tasks and events follow their natural time rather than that based upon externally imposed deadlines (Hall, 1976). *Polychronic* cultures are spread throughout the globe—far and near East, North and South America, Polynesia, Africa.

The language of a typical *polychronic* culture is characterized by an absence of past, present, and future tenses. Inferences are not drawn from the past upon which predictions of future events can be made. That is linear thinking. Time appears to be a holistic pattern into which all experiences and events are woven. In describing how the Pueblo Indian of the southwest United States fits into this model, Frank Waters (1950) states that "his life does not run on a railroad time schedule. Or between two fixed points. Sunrise and sunset, summer and winter, birth and death; within these arbitrary limits, life slowly revolves in a repetitive, timeless circle. The future does not exist. The ancient past is constantly alive. Everything is contained within the ever-living now. The Pueblo's intense awareness of this is a valid reality. Obsessed with the internal and eternal rather than the external and transient, he lives in the core of time" (p. 381). Benjamin Whorf (1956), whose linguistic research of the Hopi Pueblo Indians and their language thrust the world into a new understanding of the relation between human language and human thinking, discovered that their language contains no reference to time, either explicit or implied.

Long-term futures and pasts are recently acquired levels of human evolutionary development, and make up Fraser's *time understood* (1987). Drawing the connection with *time felt (passion time),* he observed that feelings may be independent from *time understood (knowledge time),* but not the other way around. That is, *time felt* and *time understood* are hierarchical levels of man's time bases, with time felt being the earlier, or older.

A reality built on the "internal and eternal" yet devoid of a sense of "future" does not appear to be an existence in a vacuum, but it is difficult for the Western mind to comprehend. Past, present, and future, even though they are illusions, have practical and technological value. They are the backbone of the scientific method. Linearity is necessary to test scientific hypotheses which can only be proven or rejected by plotting an accumulation of recurrences or events. The scientific method has not been achieved without a price, however. All of that questioning and probing have stripped Western man of the rich world of myth and magic. Cultures which operate in *polychronic* time appear to be more inclined toward a belief system steeped in magic and prophesy, possibly because lacking a scientific approach, fact and fantasy are not readily distinguishable (Melges, 1982).

Even as Western man takes past, present, and future for granted, there is evidence that his concept of future is shrinking as the planet shrinks, in an experiential sense, that is. In a society where technological advances are streaking by at jet speed, a future that extends even beyond tomorrow is becoming harder to hang on to, let alone to comprehend. Before a new weapons system is off the drawing board it may be obsolete. Physicians struggle to keep abreast of the latest medical wonders. The computer you bought last year is not able to handle all the fancy programs available in the current model. Children and adults alike want all their material desires fulfilled immediately. Planning for the future is often a hollow cliché (saving is even more meaningless), in spite of the fact that due to increasing life expectancies that future is growing increasingly longer. Distinct cultures are becoming endangered, being replaced by clones of the technologically sophisticated Western world. The individual is being absorbed by a social mechanism so complex that it no longer believes the human being is necessary in the organizational plan. These are symptoms of Fraser's "time-compact globe," a condition he claims will see society replace the individual as "the measure and measurer of time" (1987, p. 310). If this is so, what happens to Melges' assertion that our personal experience of time relates closely to our measure of awareness into the future. It is not beyond comprehension to perceive a time when *monochronic* time will collapse upon itself.

In most avenues of Western life, we walk easily with a future consciousness except one—education. Students receive a heavy dose of the past in all subject areas, but when the present is finally reached, time stops. "Future" is not in the core curriculum. Scholars know the past very well, and even attempt to shape the future by cleverly approaching the present. But who *knows* or is able to prepare the future? J. Samuel Bois would not restrict that backward view to formal education, but to all humanistic pursuits. Not so in technological realms, he asserts. "We accept evolution in geological and biological development and in the technical aspects of our culture, but we have not yet learned to conform our views to it when it comes to the intellectual and moral achievements of our species" (1970, p. 42). Perhaps the "future" must be given over to students themselves. Or perhaps it is necessary to feel the simultaneity of *polychronic* time to understand how to teach future time while moving in present time. "The future is purchased by the present," to quote Samuel Johnson (1969, p. 174).

The time scale we humans live on is so different from that which exists in the physical world. Each has its own temporal scale. Imagine with me, if you will, that two rocks are sitting on a table philosophizing about humankind. (They are gazing at us in our human endeavor). One rock might say to the other, "Isn't it sorrowful that their lives are so short?" A rock, in this sense, for the span of a human life tends to stay a rock, so it remains relatively stationary and unchanged to our position. Therefore, we can study it with our clock time sense and make predictions about it much more accurately. By contrast, in the behavioral sciences, the moment we impede on another person's environment, we are moving that person out of the way, and using *passion* time to do it. What we thought we could accomplish with him or her at the time we started changes because the person has also moved away from the point at which he or she started. If I want to live "long" in this world, let me be a rock!

Fraser (1987) says stones can tell us stunning tales about time, even the time of universes too alien for human life. However, their eotemporal world does not include the passage of time, even though from their view on that table they can observe a parade of generations of humans passing by. But if I want a richer life or, perhaps, reality, which allows me to experience the passage of time, complete with all the possibilities that entails, then let me remain a transient human being wandering around, often seemingly totally lost, in noetic time. Yet there is much to be learned from rocks, which the following poem by 8-year-old Craig confirms (Pearson, 1976).

> Craig, age 8 (talking about a rock)
> . . . I would be very big
> and just lie in the sun
> and get warm . . .
> . . . After millions of years I
> would have a lot of wrinkles. (pp. 43–45)

There are many different "times," not just the time we experience or have knowledge about. There are time-orders after time-orders, simply restacked. In present-day physics theory, space, time, and matter now become united into one inseparable structure that includes the whole of the physical universe. We have come to know this as Einstein's astounding theory of relativity. According to his theory, space is not three-dimensional and time is not a separate entity. There is only the space-time continuum.

In the new physics, Einstein's space-time continuum gives way to his more profound visionary concept of a unified field theory. To oversimplify, unified field theory unites the laws of gravitation and the laws of electromagnetism into one basic superstructure of universal law. Einstein did not finish this work before his death, and the physics community has not seen fit to continue where he left off. To the contrary, it claims that his unifying experiments have not contributed significantly to present-day knowledge—an evaluation not shared by the new breed of physicists—and in the words of mathematician Cornelius Lanczos (1965), "denying even the possibility of such an attempt being successful" (p. 118). Such a parochial attitude is rarely productive.

I am prompted to contradict Einstein by saying that time is not the fourth dimension but the first. In geometry, I was puzzled when it was stated that time was the fourth dimension. The teacher demonstrated the presence of a point and then would project it to get a line; the line was projected to produce a plane; the plane was projected to produce a solid. Yet it always took time to make each projection. So, we start out with time as the first experience, and everything else is built from that base. We do not talk about it exactly that way. If we could perhaps think of projecting ourselves back to a point that is supposed to have no dimensions, that might be the time we reach the speed of light. Of course, physicists are now finding that there are events faster than the speed of light, which is changing our science again.

In an attempt to refute quantum mechanics, which Einstein found too uncertain to stand as a complete theory, he, Boris Podolsky, and Nathan Rosen devised a thought experiment which proposed that if the theory of quantum mechanics was correct, the spin of one particle in a two-particle system would instantaneously affect its twin in another place. If the thought experiment could be proven, communication between the particles would travel faster than the speed of light. The very foundation of modern physics rests upon the assumption that nothing in the universe can travel faster than the speed of light, this being the law of local causes (Zukav, 1979).

The mathematical proof of the EPR effect, as the Einstein-Podolsky-Rosen thought experiment came to be known as, was achieved by J. S. Bell in 1964. This is the well-known Bell's theorem. Less than a decade later, John Clauser and Stuart Freedman confirmed that the statistical predictions of the Bell theorem were correct. But they could not show how communication between space-separated particles occurs. In a best-selling overview of the new physics aimed for the layman, Gary Zukav (1979), himself a layman, says, without question, "Bell's theorem not only suggests that the world is quite different than it seems, it demands it . . . something very exciting is happening. Physicists have 'proved,' rationally, that our rational ideas about the world in which we live are profoundly deficient" (p. 309).

Jack Sarfatti concurred, Zukav (1979) continues, when he proposed his theory of superluminal transfer of negentropy (information) without signals in 1975. Sarfatti claimed that the particles in the EPR and Clauser-Freedman experiments are separated by space and are connected, but not by signals. This connection, which is both intimate and immediate, transcends space and time.

It is well and good to recognize the evidence for such exotic ideas in the physics laboratory, but can it apply to the human experience? After all, the distinction between micro and macro sciences must be respected. Yet perhaps the connection is stronger than we suppose. For example, if you want to be with someone you love, aren't you already there?

Time and Man's Behavior (Time and Mind?)

> *"If it is true . . . that time is closely related to the rhythm*
> *of the inner god-image, the Self (i.e., the conscious-*
> *unconscious totality of the psyche), then it is obvious that*
> *every neurotic deviation from the rhythm of the Self*
> *entails also a disturbed relation to time."*

Marie-Louise von Franz,
Time: Rhythm and Repose

That assessment by von Franz asserts man's dependence on an *un*disturbed time sense for the maintenance of sound mental health.

Knowing what we do about the linkage between physical and mental health, we understand that biological clocks do not operate beyond the ken of the psyche. When physiological processes lose their normal timing and become arhythmical, the head knows. Time holds the key to normal biological operations. Likewise, psychological or inner time of the mind serves a coordinating role in mental functions, and thus is the binding medium for mental health. This is consistent with contemporary physics in the view of Larry Dossey (1982), who claims that if medical science is to fall in line with modern physical thinking, we must admit that *"time is bound to our senses*—it is part of us, it is not 'out there'" (p. 43). It is what we are. All else is elaboration *on* time, *in* time, *through* time. This means revising the accepted paradigm governing health and disease since it is dependent upon man's view of time.

Time-binding is a human characteristic not available to the other earthly levels of being. The term was originated by the distinguished philosopher-semanticist Alfred Korzybski in the 1930s. Quite literally and no less simply, to bind means to join or mix together—to cohere—to create a new compound or substance that did not previously exist. Baking bread and mixing concrete are apt examples of the binding mechanism. Man is endowed with the ability to mix, sort, retrieve, digest, and reorganize previous events, and make these available for the future. Not so for the animal, plant, and mineral levels of being which must start each "generation" anew with a blank slate. The experience of past generations is available to man alone, allowing him to build and call upon a repository of information about himself and his environment. This is then passed on to succeeding generations. Time-binding, thus, allows civilizations to develop, agriculture and technology to be invented, governmental systems to be designed, that is to say, time-binding orders voluntary and intentional change to occur.

Before we pursue time as the binding medium for mental health, we need to understand the brain's role in all of this (see "On Music, Mind, Education, and Human Development," "Man's Brains," Chapter 4). The brain is a highly specialized time-binding organ. Although it is an organ of specialized functions, there is no single area primarily responsible for timing and temporal processes. Different areas seem to involve themselves in temporal processing in different ways. First, however, it must be understood that the human brain is a self-organizing system consisting of three units—the reptilian brain, the mammalian (or paleomammalian) brain, and the cerebral cortex (or neomammalian) brain. Each "brain," or unit, represents a major evolutionary leap in the development of the human species. While viewing and analyzing each separately will serve to expand understanding of the brain, per se, it must be understood that these three units function as a single, interrelated, intermeshing whole.

The most primitive of the three units, the reptilian brain, has a limited temporal capacity, involved mostly in biological rhythms. The mammalian brain, which is of more recent evolutionary origin, can handle longer time periods (Melges, 1982). This exceedingly complex and little understood unit of the brain is also known as the limbic system. It is involved with such diverse functions as emotions, feelings, attention, memory, and learning sensations which we often erroneously prescribe exclusively to the human species. Temporal involvement exists to a limited extent in all these functions, but none so strongly as in the area of memory. For our present purposes, the hippocampus is the most relevant component of the limbic system, for it allows selective attention to only what is important among the mass of stimuli that constantly bombard the human nervous system, playing the same role in recall of stored information. Without this critical selectivity, long- and short-term memory could not be separated from the present, and for all practical purposes, we would be without memory (Rand McNally, 1976). And finally, the cerebral cortex, which is the sophisticated human brain, is the most highly developed, dealing with the more complex issues of time.

Breaking down the functions of the cerebral cortex further, we note that the left and right hemispheres appear to process time relationships differently. The left hemisphere is primarily sequential, the right largely simultaneous. Once again we encounter our friends *knowledge time* and *passion time*, respectively. However, let us not forget that the corpus callosum, that bridge which joins the two hemispheres, allows rapid exchange of stimuli between the hemispheres. Why this duplication? Melges suggests that processing information both sequentially and simultaneously might enhance anticipation—i.e., future time. Seeing a multitude of sequences simultaneously may allow a person a longer sense of future. Time is such a powerful force, so it would seem, that the brain gives over much of its space to temporal processing. Although our knowledge of the brain is limited, and even what is known keeps changing, there can be little doubt that time is central to its functioning, ranging from conditioning to planning.

If psychological time is central to mental health, then does it not follow that its (time) distortion contributes to mental illness? The causes of personal time distortion are too numerous to chronicle, but whatever they are, once distortion occurs, psychological reality is affected and consciousness is altered. It is as though personal reality follows whatever temporal road map is offered up by the cerebral cortex. We follow that map and from it gain our personal identity and temporal perspective. Put another way, "the sense of identity is related to the continuity of temporal perspective, particularly future time perspective . . . [and] that temporal disintegration appears to induce depersonalization . . ." (Melges, 1990, p. 265).

Continuing with Melges' (1990) views on temporal perspective, he believes that temporal distortions manifest themselves in a variety of psychiatric syndromes. That is, the "disorganized thinking" and "misconstrued expectations" manifest in mental illness may be the result of, or, at the very least, involved in the temporal disorganization of the mind. This disorder can be identified as disorganization of sequence, rate, and/or temporal perspective, which are the basic components of psychological time. It follows then that restoring temporal order should be the overarching treatment goal. Does it not further follow that the most appropriate treatment medium should be temporal in character? Music is the best example, to my mind, for it addresses directly rate, sequence, and temporal perspective, these being the basic components of music as well as psychological time. We now turn to music to determine how these components can be utilized in treatment.

Music—the Art of Time

Gotthold Ephraim Lessing, the 18th century German philosopher-dramatist, opined that music is the art of time. If time is the primary "geometric structure" which unifies the universe (with a little help from space and matter), then is not music the unifying art? Fraser (1975) considers music to be the ultimate of the arts—of expression, really—and that the most striking effect the temporal arts exert on man is a sense of transcending time.

If music both transcends time and *is* time, are not both Fraser's *passion* and *knowledge* times required for music's existence? To explore this question further, four positions taken in the original discussion of "music demands time-ordered behavior" (Sears, 1968) will be examined. These are:

1.   Music cannot be interrupted without losing its intent
2.   The necessity for moment-to-moment commitment by the individual rests in the music itself
3.   Time-order extends beyond rhythm
4.   The tempos of life and music are comparable

Music cannot be interrupted. You are listening to a favorite musical selection on your stereo and the telephone rings. You are forced to direct your attention away from the music and toward the voice on the other end of the line. In this minor disruption, more has occurred than the simple interruption of a pleasurable experience. A psychological process has been short-circuited, and the future is different from what it would have been had you been able to listen to the end of the piece. Music must be completed in a single "sitting" to carry any meaning. The sequence of events must occur in predictable succession, one upon the other, uninterrupted. For the neurotic patient who is unable to plan ahead, music can crumble the time disorientation in which he/she is trapped. Its time-ordered component is so obvious to us that we forget the power inherent in it. One can mutilate the time-order of a musical experience just so far before it becomes something else.

Experiencing the present moment and going into the future is unique to music. Time is the major difference between music and the other arts. Dance probably comes the closest to being a temporal art, although this is more because it moves in musical time, whether or not accompanied by music. Dance addresses itself principally to the visual sense, and thus belongs to the world of space. However, by Suzanne Langer's reasoning (1953), the space of dance is always illusory—a created element. That is, the space (and time, as well) in which dance exists is not actual, but rather, virtual.

There is another element of dance which we must recognize and that Fraser (1987) terms "the ecstasy of the dance." It is created from the rhythmic motion upon which the dancer's feelings are focused. But, and this is the crux of Fraser's point, this steady beat "has no preferred direction in time, just as the ticks of the clock do not; . . . it is the absence of temporal direction that the dancer notices" (p. 296–297). Yet another oddity found in the "psyche" of the dance is that while dance is a temporal art, it can become frozen in time. What a conundrum!

Even drama and poetry can be interrupted, slowed down, or speeded up. A book is read chapter by chapter and usually is put aside several times before completed. We can look at paintings from the top corner down, from the side to the middle—any way we choose, any time we choose, and for as long as we choose. We may better understand the message being transmitted through the artist's centering cues, and maybe in most instances we are automatically drawn to the center. However, this is not required in order to see, actually experience, the picture the artist has produced. We can come back tomorrow and find for all of our lives the same picture.

We can modify or change our methods of experiencing other arts media. But music is so basic a process, enjoying a direct channel to the temporal lobe within the cerebral cortex without the need of transformation or conversion from its original state, that the moment we commit ourselves to it, we must be ordered in our behavior to some point in the future if meaning is to result and reality prevail. You cannot stop the music capriciously, or put it aside, and end up with anything but disparate tones. It is this driving force, an adventure into the future, and the idea of being successful and safe in the adventure that creates a unique personal contact music therapists enjoy with their clients. Nothing else that I know of in life is as temporally ordered. I think this is so basic that we cannot even ask the right questions about what it means. We bypass it and insist upon the right pitches, pleasing tone qualities, and strict tempi. Yes, George Bernard Shaw was correct—the most difficult question to answer is the one to which the answer is apparent.

Earlier I stated that distortions of personal time are a primary cause of mental illness. Persons usually are hospitalized because they mishandle the time-ordering of their society, and disorganized thinking results. Thus, to restore mental health, a major therapeutic approach is to help people handle time by removing the causes for the time distortions which plague them. How to remove the time distortions which are firmly engrained? It stands to reason that the treatment of choice should be temporally grounded, which, of course, aptly describes music. The temporal demands inherent in music are quite subtle. We are not aware in the act of music-making that our behavior is being strictly engineered. By attending to the music, which is the "now," behavior becomes socially acceptable, and there is no room for time distortions. Thus, each time an individual successfully "sees" a musical selection through to completion, ordered time is being reinforced.

Moment-to-moment commitment rests in the music itself. The notion of time-order starts when the patient is introduced to the music, and he/she is immediately, although subtly, confronted with him- or herself. For some patients, such as those suffering from affective disorders, committing to anything that extends over time provokes stress because of their disorganized concept of rate or duration of events. However, the music totally determines duration of the commitment, and gradually the time interval committed to the activity is elongated. But the process does not end there. In fact, it does not even begin there, but rather with the music itself as it exists through time in the environment. Time-order is the "stuff" of which music is made. It is a fundamental element of the medium. Take a single drumbeat, increase the speed and a tone will start to emerge. Add a few syncopations to the beat, and a complex tone results. From complex tones and combinations of higher orders of time-order, harmony is produced. Slow down the impulse a bit, and the result is rhythm. All kinds of manipulations are possible with time.

Perhaps the most powerful manipulation is the sense of motion built into the music that propels it on into the future and makes the human commitment ironclad. Epstein (1981) believes such motion must be purposeful—controlled and directed—as the composer creates, and that without this, music does not work, "lacking the 'glue' of real-time flow that binds these parts into coherent movements, composed and heard from beginning to end" (p. 186). It is almost as though the composer—and eventually the performer—must be conscious of the time factor in music, and must manipulate it in such a fashion that the listener will be compelled to stay with the music until completed.

In *Sound and Symbol,* Victor Zuckerkandl (1956) presents a compelling discussion of time in music. He claims that time in music is not a "mere formality;" it is the "force." That is, time is the energy, the power that *is* music. He even goes beyond this by stating that if force were omitted from the discussion about music, there would be little left to describe. Force is no less real than is music itself. Time is not an abstraction—an empty vessel into which tones, rhythm, and harmony are poured. No, he asserts, time becomes solid experiential content through tones. Even that assertion could be challenged if it were not for the rest—musical silence. If tones are omitted and time is filled with silence, "what remains is not abstract, empty form but a highly concrete experience; the experience of rhythm. There would be no rhythm if time could not be experienced as such, in itself" (p. 203).

And what of that moment of silence that precedes the opening attack? Lewis Rowell (1981) believes that this period of "no time" is an important preparation for the new time (music) which is to come. "It is a highly artificial, tensed silence," he writes, "a way of erasing our previous consciousness of time and of external events, a period of intense focus, concentration, and pure expectation during which we are poised on the brink of time, as it were, and are made ready to process the rapid succession of temporal clues we are about to receive" (p. 201). Yes, silence is also in the music, and its only medium of expression is time. Arthur Schnabel (Peter, 1977) also recognized the weight of silence in music when he said, "The notes I handle no better than many pianists. But the pauses between the notes—ah, that is where the art resides!" (p. 350). I must wonder how many artists and listeners have the remotest understanding of the enormity of this seemingly radical statement, and more importantly, whether they appreciate the virtue of silence in music.

At this point, it may be tempting to extend this discourse to other properties of music which affect the personal commitment. Surely, the melodic line drives the listener on. Meter provides an overarching organization, and harmony is both foundation and movement. Yet we have not digressed from the basic theme of time-order. We cannot separate the basic elements of music into temporal and nontemporal components. Music *is* temporality. Zuckerkandl (1956) maintains that "there is hardly a phenomenon that can tell us more about time and temporality than can music" (p. 152). Thus, the above examples should suffice for our present purposes.

We cannot point to anything in the environment which gives music its reality. By its very nature, music provides its own reality, not being dependent upon external forces for meaning. Of course, the ideas, the imaginings which the composer weaves into his work may be drawn from the environment, but they are not one and the same with the resultant musical product. Music is constructed from a purely dynamic nature, not a static object. The laws of music do not dictate the course of events, but instead show the way, allowing free choice of the path taken. All of this reinforces what a powerful tool music id, not only for therapy but also equally for so-called normal and maybe cosmic relationships.

Time order extends beyond rhythm. When the statement, "*time order*, as conceived here, is a broader concept than rhythm" (Sears, 1968, p. 35) was written in the mid-1960s, it may have been erroneously implied that the prevailing opinion of the day credited music's temporality primarily to rhythm. Nothing could be further from the truth, as was explained later in that paragraph. Yet the mere fact of its prominence there implies the importance we have placed on rhythm's temporal power.

Most listeners usually do not object when a slight mistake in a musical rendition is made. No one objects, that is, except musicians, who have been trained to care, to object, and to criticize. The one exception is that most people are bothered by rhythmic errors. Perhaps you have attended a church whose organist decides, for some reason, that the last chord before the hymn commences should be held longer than the tempo indicates. The introduction is played, the congregation is prepared to sing, but the organist is not. Or listening to a very familiar selection performed either too slow or too fast for the tempo we feel is correct. We cannot be given three beats in proper tempo and then be made to wait for the fourth without experiencing some discomfort because the normal expectancies have been interrupted. We need to perceive that time is flowing clockwise in equally measured cadence, not by fits and starts. This time-ordered behavior is the feeling state that works so powerfully for music therapy. Time is so "in" us. Man has yet to devise a verbal system which makes cognitive sense out of time, but somehow we go ahead and substitute in our heads the reality and feeling for which there are no words. The interruption of time bothers us more than anything else. Patients experiencing acute psychosis often have lost their temporal perspective. Time span has no coherence. The melodic and rhythmic demands of music can provide a strong therapeutic tool for correcting this temporal disintegration.

From the beginning of our musical studies, we have been taught specific keyboard fingerings. Many of us must continually look back and forth from fingers to musical notes because we never learned the importance of time. The only reason for the instruction book is to remind us of certain rules and techniques. However, we make the book more important than the sound we produce. We concentrate more on playing the right key than on the musical line moving through time. If this is the system by which we were taught and we do not advance beyond technical facility, we end up time butcherers instead of musicians. Yet this is not an altogether accurate explanation of how we "learn" music, as [the late] Julian Jaynes (1976) asserts in his powerful work, *The Origin of Consciousness in the Breakdown of the Bicameral Mind,* the title of which is almost as lengthy as is his message. Jaynes uses piano-playing as a fitting example of the role consciousness plays in mental functioning. To move beyond butchering time and to actually reproduce the music on the printed page, consciousness fades into the background. It is literally impossible to be mentally aware of all the tasks required to play even a simple musical piece. Certainly, we must focus on these when learning the piece, but once beyond that, consciousness is only fleetingly involved, if at all.

The sense of temporality is embodied in tone. It is even arguable to assert that before rhythm comes tone, notwithstanding that musical rhythm enjoys a much longer history. Returning again to Zuckerkandl's admirable treatise on the meaning of time in music (1956), he explains that even before tone succeeds to melody the sense of movement exists, a concept that has been expressed by others, such as Fraser (1975, 1987), Epstein (1981), and Rowell (1981). It is not only that clock time passes as a tone is sounded, but the need to move on in order to encounter completeness is built into tone. A tone demands completion, which means, quite literally, to cease being and let something else—something that is still in the future—

happen. The moment a tone sounds, time is opened to the listener, that is, tone draws the listener to time. The tone is the present striving to become the past so that the future can be. More will be said about past, present, and future in the following sections.

To ignore any discussion of melody when speaking of tone denies the relationship that exists between the two. However, a survey of the psychology of music is beyond the scope of the present argument. Suffice it to say, melody is organized sound which conveys meaning to a body of people, and further, that such meaning is bound to cultural bonds among people. Without this cultural unity, the result would be a parade of disparate tones through time.

Harmony has some features which upon first glance appear to be time-exempt. The structure of harmony is vertical. The notes of a chord usually, although not always, appear simultaneously in time. Although we do not deny that chordal progression, which creates harmony, is no less temporal than all other musical elements, it is this frozen-in-time character of the chord that is troubling. Nor is it valid to compare the tone/melody development with the chord/harmony one. The difference appears to be the dynamic quality inherent in a single chord which is absent from a lone tone. There is something about the union of several tones, devoid of any outside influence, that produces a dynamic sense and creates harmonic motion. Thus, harmony best exemplifies the marriage of simultaneity and time.

Melody, harmony, meter, timbre, dynamics—all are time-ordered. Frequency or pitch is a measure of cyclic time. Melody and harmony become linear time. Formal structure of musical phrases are longer extensions of linear time. The overtone series expresses compounded time frequencies. Within music there exists the greatest collection of multiplicities of time experience, appealing simultaneously to both the conscious and unconscious. This, in Fraser's mind (1975), is why music is the "art of arts." Whatever organizations exist in music, time-order is the underlying factor—the constancy in a sea of change.

Tempos of life and music are comparable. Fraser (1975) speaks of the "duality of time-in-music versus the time-of-life and the harmony of dissonance between the two . . ." (p. 408). Von Franz (1978) recognized the uniqueness of music when she said, "Man could be called a complex living clock. In dance and music we express the rhythmicity of our whole structure—these are arts through which we relate to time and give it meaning" (p. 87). Langer (1953) states that music creates an order of "virtual time," that is, an intangible, illusory image. It exists in experiential or "lived" time, Fraser's *passion time.* Yet it becomes a perfect substitute for clock time. Humans are not endowed with time perception nor a time consciousness, only an awareness of *change.* Of course, change itself is not an observable event that can be sensorily experienced but rather a series of "states" contrasting with one another. Change creates time. Zuckerkandl (1956) says this is not so for the music listener who observes that change does *not* create time; rather, it is the other way, time creates change!

My own interpretation of all this is that music seems to happen to us at about the speed that we feel life is moving. At times it may coincide with clock time, while at other times will be totally experiential. Even this speed is not exclusively a product of *passion time,* but is influenced by the music itself—musical time, as it were. It is tempo that alters perception of time. Time appears to move fast when listening or performing a musical selection which contains many notes in close periodic sequence and which is texturally rich. Conversely, if there are few notes which are drawn out over a long period, time perception is extended. In these ways, it can be seen that music, in fact, structures time.

Langer (1953) put this thought into more scholarly terms by declaring that:

> music spreads out time for our direct and complete apprehension, by letting our hearing monopolize it—organize, fill, and shape it, *all alone* [italics added]. It creates an image of time measured by the motion of forms that seem to give it substance, yet a substance that consists entirely of sound, so it is transitoriness itself. *Music makes time audible, and its form and continuity sensible* [italics added]. (p. 110)

And, it must be noted, of the five physical senses, only hearing has direct knowledge of time.

> Subjectively, time has a fluid quality which much resembles a running brook; sometimes bubbling past in a furious rush, sometimes slipping by quietly unnoticed, and sometimes lying languid, almost stationary, in deep pools. (Zukav, 1979, p. 170)[1]

---

[1] Editor's Note: In the course of organizing this section, I came across an article written by the late MIT professor David Epstein in 1981. In it he expressed ideas that W. Sears had espoused as far back as 1964. A brief example is appropriate at this juncture. To quote Epstein, music "is a temporal art in which flow, structure, and continuity are essential. However, no . . . flexibility in its performance could be taken by musicians . . . [as is possible with other arts forms] without wholesale distortion of the musical text. In this sense music is perhaps unique not only among the arts but in our experience of time itself. . . . Music actually *structures* time—and the flow of time—in precise quanta and proportions, controlling this flow, its intensities, its direction, its speed, its goal orientation, to a degree unmatched in other domains of our temporal experience" (p. 182).

The speed with which we go into the future is where most of us encounter difficulty, especially if we are still learning our craft. Psychological problems usually develop in people who have lost control of their futures and who cannot function within the flow of time dictated by their society. We have to move into the future at about the same speed with music as we live our lives. This reinforces my earlier remark. It is very crucial that we understand this in order to comprehend what is happening in the musical situation, and how to transfer this to the therapeutic setting. In other words, the time-order which is built into music must match our internal clocks to a degree that will allow us to cope with all the vicissitudes life spreads before us—the greater the match, the stronger our coping techniques.

This "times" match is Altshuler's Iso-principle (1948), a homeostatic concept which prescribes that the affective character of the music be in equal, or "iso" relation to that of the listener-client. At the outset, the music is selected to match the client's mood. Gradually, the mood of the music is altered to bring about a changed and more appropriate behavior in the listener. Sadly, the Iso-principle is rarely referred to by name these days, yet the process is used by some music therapists even though they may not be aware of its history. If therapists would be made aware of the intrinsic value of the Iso-principle, and used it regularly as a clinical technique, music therapy would be strengthened. The Iso-principle is one tool in the music therapist's arsenal. It should be used, it should be written about, and most importantly, it should be examined and tested. Until that occurs, we will never know its true value. Actually, a form of the Iso-prinicple is regularly applied when therapists obtain musical preference information from their patients as part of the patient assessment battery.

Finding the client's inner clock and determining how far it is from what is acceptable to society and what is necessary to satisfactorily function in that society, becomes the therapist's task. However, we must understand also that people can and do run on different times, societal dictates notwithstanding, and recognize that they are able to handle exceptions to

---

"*Music structures time*" claims Epstein (and a few other renown scholars), not the other way around. Essentially, this has been the premise of this chapter. Even "music as time-ordered behavior" presupposes that time-order is implicit in music, serving at the pleasure of the flowing music. Can we exchange "creates" for "structures" in the above Epstein quotation? It certainly follows, but what happens if "exists in" is substituted? This turns the thesis around and removes the power of music which exists because of its direct connection to the emotive self. No intermediary is necessary, or more precisely, occurs between the aural source (ear) and the interpretive center (brain).

their individual times much of the time. This is being demonstrated more and more by business and industry, which will allow employees whose work does not depend upon a set time schedule to determine the time period they choose to work. This is called "flextime."

Polychronic cultures, as was explained earlier, perceive time as a patterned whole rather than proceeding linearly through past, present, and future. Yet even *monochronic* cultures as our own cannot scientifically sort out the distinction. For example, in geophysical clock time "now" is relatively unimportant. In fact, there is no such thing as the present. There is a little bit of time between the stimulus of "now" and the time the observer can conceive of it or perceive it, as I discovered in high school geometry. Therefore, we are always operating in the past.

Physicist David Bohm's description of this phenomenon (Weber, 1982) goes something like this: the past is contained in the present in the form of memory, and the future is projected from the present as a response of memory. If the present is the dividing line between past and future, which do not actually exist as such, then, Bohm asserts, the present also cannot exist. This leaves us with an "unspecifiable" and "indescribable" present. Another conundrum! However, all is not chaos; since we know that the present recurs regularly based on the past, we can be fairly confident that the pattern will continue.

This can relate to musical processes such as the speed with which we perform music, the way we practice, and even our listening styles, all of which are found in the therapy session. The object of the practice, by following this concept, would be to try to make the future coincide more closely with the present moment. In other words, when we are learning a piece of music, we practice slowly, and then speed up as we become more familiar with it through numerous repetitions. We are, in a sense, trying to make the future coincide more closely with the present, which we are never able to do because by the time we have awareness of the present moment, it has already passed.

All of the profound statements made through the ages do not compare with Bois' (1966) down-to-earth logic about the origin of the meaning of the concept "present." The present exists sandwiched between past and future, he says, "because somebody created it as a pattern of thinking about a process-happening that had no definite place, borders, or size. Somebody put it there long, long ago. Once the thinking pattern was invented and put into circulation, nobody thought of inventing a different one to modify our reaction to that process-happening" (p. 158). It is as simple as that! If Bois' assessment is true, one must wonder what earth-shattering problems were so consuming the minds of the great thinkers through the ages that they could not energize their exceptional cerebral endowments to tackle the "present" question.

Musical memory also has a part to play in this temporal drama. Roger Jones (1982) wonders in what state is a musical work held in memory by the listener thoroughly familiar with the piece? "It is not in time as in a performance, any more than our ideas, recollections, and dreams may be thought of as existing in objective time. . . . The apprehension of a piece of music, held as a totality in the memory, gives us a glimpse of a different kind of time consciousness . . . , in which experiences are not sequential . . . , but are simultaneous, and amalgamated into an organic complex" (p. 92–93). What may have (or may not have, for that matter) entered the head in Fraser's *knowledge time* now is transformed into a holistic pattern where linearity is a stranger.

Time is our problem. If we could forget everything bad that has happened to us and not project it into the future, we would be safe. It is not the present moment—however abstract that concept may be—that bothers us so much as worrying about what happened in the past, and what that may have to do with the future. The objective in music therapy is to start in the present—where it is not hurting—move into the future, and make whatever has been troubling us not happen sooner. Maybe we even can forget about it. Thus, through music we are led to an absence of memory.

In the course of [writing this chapter], I discovered numerous statements scholars have written about the mysteries of *time*, aside from complete volumes written by such persons as J. T. Fraser. Many statements were so profound that paraphrasing seemed an injustice to the depth of thinking that produced them. It would have been simple to string these quotations together, and thus create a coherent and logical argument. Short of that, I can only hope that I have piqued the curiosity of the [reader] to search out the original sources and delve deeper into the astounding world of time*s*.

Editor's Summary

This chapter's premise that music is time-ordered behavior was tested by exploring the meaning of time and the temporal nature of music. Time cannot be expressed or even experienced in the singular, but instead exists in many different states, both linear and nonlinear. Cultures, and even individual human beings, operate on different time scales, demonstrating the multiplicity of temporalities. Then there is the time of physics, which had been successfully avoided until Einstein forced the issue in the early 20th century.

Man's inner time is also a hierarchy of temporalities. How smart the brain must be to keep track of all those ticking biological and psychological clocks, thereby assuring that harmony reigns in the system. When asynchrony develops, particularly in the psychological time pieces, mental and physical health is jeopardized. Indeed, temporal distortion is a leading cause of mental illness.

Music is the art of time. All of its elements—individually and collectively—are the embodiment of temporality. Yet music also has the ability to transcend time. We must thus say that music is endowed with its own music-time *(knowledge time)* and listener/performer-time *(passion time)*. Music is a multiplicity of temporalities. Thus, we must conclude that music is time*s*-ordered behavior.

References

Altshuler, I. M. (1948). A psychiatrist's experience with music as a therapeutic agent. In D. M. Schullian & M. Schoen (Eds.), *Music and Medicine*. New York: Henry Schuman.

Alexander, E. (1956). Germany-philosophy (23). In *The Encyclopedia Americana* (Vol. 12). New York: Americana.

Barwick, D. D. (1970). *Great words of our time*. Kansas City, MO: Hallmark Editions.

Bois, J. S. (1966). *The art of awareness*. Dubuque, IA: William C. Brown.

Bois, J. S. (1970). *Breeds of men*. New York: Harper & Row.

Dossey, L. (1982). *Space, time and medicine*. Boulder, CO: Shambhala.

Epstein, D. (1981). On musical continuity. In J. T. Fraser (Ed.) *The Study of Time IV*. New York: Springer.

Fraser, J. T. (1975). *Of time, passion, and knowledge*. Princeton, NJ: Princeton University Press.

Fraser, J. T. (1987). *Time, the familiar stranger*. Redmond, WA: Tempus Books.

Hall, E. T. (1976). *Beyond culture*. New York: Anchor/Doubleday.

Herodotus: The Histories. (1972). (A. de Sélincourt, Trans.). London: Penguin Books.

Jaynes, J. (1976). *The origin of consciousness in the breakdown of the bicameral mind*. Boston: Houghton Mifflin Company.

Johnson, S. (1969). Many advantages not to be enjoyed together, essay #178. In W. J. Bate & A. B. Strauss (Eds.), *The rambler: Vol. 5. Yale edition of the works of Samuel Johnson*. New Haven, CT: Yale University Press.

Jones, R. S. (1982). *Physics as metaphor*. Minneapolis: University of Minnesota Press.

Keen, S. & Fox, A. V. (1973). *Telling your story: A guide to who you are and who you can be*. New York: The New American Library.

Kramer, J. D. (1988). *The time of music: New meanings, new temporalities, new listening strategies.* New York: Schirmer Books.

Lanczos, C. (1965). *Albert Einstein and the cosmic world order.* New York: John Wiley & Sons.

Langer, S. (1953). *Feeling and form.* New York: Charles Scribner's Sons.

Melges, F. T. (1982). *Time and the inner future: A temporal approach to psychiatric disorders.* New York: John Wiley & Sons.

Melges, F. T. (1990) Identity and temporal perspectives. In Richard A. Black (Ed.), *Cognitive models of psychological time.* Hillsdale, NJ: Erlbaum Associates.

Pearson, J. (1976). *Begin sweet world.* Garden City, NY: Doubleday.

Peter, L. J. (1977). *Peters' quotations.* New York: William Morrow.

Rand McNally. (1976). *Atlas of the body and mind.* New York: Rand McNally & Company.

Rowell, L. (1981). The creation of audible time. In J. T. Fraser (Ed.) *The study of time IV.* New York: Springer.

Sears, W. W. (1968). Processes in music therapy. In E. T. Gaston (Ed.), *Music in therapy.* New York: Macmillan.

Toffler, A. (1970). *Future shock.* New York: Random House.

von Franz, M. (1978). *Time: Rhythm and repose.* London: Thames & Hudson.

Waters, F. (1950). *Masked gods.* New York: Ballantine Books.

Weber, R. (1982). The enfolding-unfolding universe: A conversation with David Bohm. In K. Wilber (Ed.), *The holographic paradigm.* Boulder, CO: Shambhala.

Whorf, B. (1956). *Language, thought, and reality.* New York: John Wiley & Sons.

Zuckerkandl, V. (1956). *Sound and symbol.* Princeton, NJ: Princeton University Press.

Zukav, G. (1979). *Dancing Wu Li masters.* New York: William Morrow.

Chapter Seven

Semantic and Existential Implications for Music Therapy

We have thousands of descriptions of emotional disturbance and its causes. But we have few descriptions of emotional health. And so, as I say, what does a sane person look like?

S. I. Hayakawa, *Symbol, Status, and Personality*

Life is not a having and a getting, but a being and a becoming.

Matthew Arnold

Editor's Introduction

All that remains of this speech are the author's notes, which are incomplete. It is presumed, although not confirmed, that this speech was presented at the April 1962 conference of the Great Lakes regional chapter of the National Association for Music Therapy.

Sears was an ecumenical scholar, esoteric in a humbling and complimentary way. He readily invited persons to join in his love of learning and mental exploration, whether they were ready for it or not. Early in our relationship, he eagerly tried to pique my interest in the late P. D. Ouspensky (1878–1947), the Russian giant philosopher whose *Tertuim Organum* (1911) became a best-seller and established his reputation worldwide. Well, I tell you, I so much wanted to impress Bill, but once past Ouspensky's prefatory material, my concentration level nose-dived significantly. Many years later, I admitted that if I had stuck with it long enough to engage Bill in discussion about Ouspensky's ideas, he would have explained these to me in his special clear thinking style, and I would have been the wiser.

Presenting complex topics in a coherent, plain-spoken, and unambiguous manner which engaged the listener was one of Bill's special talents. Unfortunately, that did not happen with me and Ouspensky. However, in a very real fashion, this chapter expresses the core of Bill's creed, that being to share with others one's excitement for discovering different, perhaps remote ideas by engaging them in conversation.

Knowledge is useless unless one gives it away. It is not my intent to imply that others have not seen a connection between existentialism and general semantics and music therapy, but rather that Bill did, and presented his ideas to his colleagues.

History of General Semantics and Existentialism

The study of semantics and existentialism as they apply in psychology, psychoanalysis, psychotherapy, and psychiatry are relatively recent developments. Semantics as a discipline came into being early in the 20th century. It is concerned with the systematic study of meaning. General semantics was introduced by Alfred Korzybski in 1933 in his monumental work, *Science and Sanity*. The International Society for General Semantics (Chase, 1954) has concisely defined it as "the study and improvement of human evaluative processes with special emphasis on the relation to signs and symbols, including language" (p. 128). It differs from semantics in its emphasis on mathematics, neurology, relativity, and psychology. More succinctly, in S. I. Hayakawa's view (1963), general semantics "is the study of what makes human beings human" (p. vi), and sometimes, when symbolism becomes distorted, less than human.

Korzybski's theories have been somewhat modified over the years. Some names of significance are S. I. Hayakawa, Anatol Rapoport, Richard Dettering, Wendell Johnson, and Stuart Chase. The people in general semantics represent many professional fields.

The *Comprehensive Textbook of Psychiatry* (Reedman, Kaplan, & Sadock, 1975) defines existential psychotherapy as being based on existential philosophy which reckons that man alone is responsible for his existence. This therapy emphasizes "confrontation, primarily in the here-and-now interaction, and on feeling experiences, rather than on rational thinking. Little attention is given to patient resistances" (p. 2585). Both therapist and patient are involved on the *same level* and to the *same degree.*

Rollo May is one of the most notable exponents of existential psychology in the United States. Other persons who agree with its concepts include Gordon Allport, Abraham Maslow, and Carl Rogers. Existential psychology claims international followers among Freudian analysts such as V. E. von Gebstattel, Medard Boss, Ludwig Binswanger, and Gustave Bally, and among psychiatrists and neurologists such as Eugene Minkowski, Erwin Straus, and R. D. Laing.

A philosopher friend of mine was somewhat puzzled when I mentioned the topic of this paper. He wondered how existentialism and semantics could be combined. This combination could be only my peculiar twist of ideas. Yet the two subjects seem to be concerned with somewhat the same problems, even though each provides a different verbal formulation, and their postulates can be found in music therapy.

The development of formulations in both semantics and existential psychology is still taking place. As seen here, both semantics and existential psychology are not striving to take their places along with the formulations of Freud, Jung, Adler, Horney, Sullivan, and the like. Rather, they are attempting to get at an understanding of the underlying structure of man's existence and functioning. They are related to the other formulations much like a pure or basic science is to its own applied science. They more or less represent attitudes and assumptions about man upon which applied therapy techniques must be designed.

The presentation here will, of necessity, be rather sketchy, but hopefully detailed enough so as not to stir up any false misinterpretations of the implications these studies have for our own therapeutic approaches. It borrows heavily from respected authorities in both disciplines. Also, this will be a presentation of some "first thoughts," and should be judged as such.

For some time I have been troubled by the fact that even after all of these years there still exists a large chasm between music therapy theory and practice. The questions "What is music therapy?' and "What is the therapy in music therapy?" continue to plague us in spite of increased sophistication and knowledge within the profession. Some of the same answers are being given today as were given ten years ago; yet, it seems that none of us know the answers when asked. We talk about what music does to people, and can support our claims with research data, but struggle to express with any certitude just how one must go about arranging the milieu which will achieve what is claimed. We talk all around the point, then finally, in desperation, we take the inquirers into an experience. Whatever goes on in that experience, the way we present it, is what we are trying to talk about, but the words will not suffice. However, to reach those beyond the sound of our voice, we must use words, so we need to learn to translate that mysterious, magical, real something—whatever it is—into verbal language. In practice, we seem to operate on the premise that all we need to do is put patients into music therapy and changes will occur.

Existential Psychology

Existential psychology is concerned with basic assumptions about man, the human being. It takes its meaning from the root word "existence," which stems from the Latin *ex-sistere*, defined as "to emerge or stand out." Thus, existential psychology deals with the state of becoming (being-in-the-world), emphasizing man's coming into being. This is the classic textbook definition which reads verbatim in almost all scholarly writings on the subject. Now, I have a bit of a problem understanding exactly what the existentialists mean by "existence," "being," "being in the world," and all those other catchy definitional statements. But I have no difficulty comprehending that existential psychology is aimed at getting back to life itself, which comes from Abraham Maslow (1966). To put a decidedly graphic interpretation to this statement, visualize, if you will, a person caught in mid-air while leaping into a pond. The ground surrounding the pond is labeled "spectator," while the word "participant" is spread across the water. So long as I can retain that concrete image in my head, I am better able to understand the complexities of existential psychology.

These basic assumptions about man constitute "pictures in the head," perhaps not too different from my visual definition. It is, in a sense, a formulation of attitudes about the nature of man, rather than a special school or system of therapy, and should precede the standard psychological systems. It "does not deny the validity of the study of dynamisms and patterns of behavior in their rightful places, but it holds that drives or dynamisms, by whatever name they may be called, can be understood only in the context of the structure of the existence of the given, particular person with whom we are dealing" (May, 1959, p. 1352)—the patient as he/she appears before the therapist.

Admittedly, one cannot discuss existentialism without referring to "being," for the goal of existential psychology is not to effect a cure, although that is okay, but rather to help the patient fulfill his "being." Better stated in May's words (1959), the intent is that the patient "experience his existence as real, and experience it fully, which includes experiencing his potentialities and being able to act on the basis of them" (p. 1358). Notice, May uses "experience" in the verb transitive form three times in one sentence, reinforcing the sense of action. Traditional therapy, by contrast, often is aimed more toward helping the patient adjust to the culture, that is, live a well-organized, orderly life. "Being" and "experiencing" can get lost in such an approach.

You might see what happens to yourself if you put aside such thoughts as, "There is the patient," and "Here am I, the therapist," and in its place substitute the idea, saying it to yourself, as it were, "Here we are, two people making music together, each contributing what we can by truly participating in each other." With the latter attitude, we invite *direct* knowledge and a more vigorous sense of reality into the process, going beyond the artificiality often found in traditional psychotherapy, and the patient becomes alive to us.

One of the hazards of the therapeutic professions is an excessive concentration on knowledge *about* the patient, as evidenced by the lengthy case records hospitals require, while *direct* knowledge through the encounter between therapist and patient has been left to chance. Existential psychology places great store in the experience of encounter, de-emphasizing technique (May, 1959). Patient and therapist become existential partners, sharing "the totality of existence." The therapist must "be-in-the-world" with the patient, that is, "be together with him in all phases of his total experience" (Ruitenbeek, 1962, p. xxi).

Existentialism is currently clouded in uncertainty and confusion in May's view (1961), "associated as it is with the beatnik movement at one extreme and with esoteric, untranslatable, Germanic, philosophical concepts at the other. True also, the movement collects the 'lunatic fringe' groups—to which existential psychology and psychiatry are by no means immune" (p. 18). Yet centering upon the existing person, which is basic to existentialism, has both contemporary and historical validity, thereby saving it from degradation. May goes so far as to say that every good psychotherapist is existential in that he is able "to grasp the patient in his reality" (p. 19).

However, more revealing to me is May's excellent critical examination of "Existential Therapy and the American Scene" (1967). He claims that the best metaphor for the contemporary American character can be found in the features associated with the "frontier." We are only several generations removed from the westward geographical migration, an attitude still deeply engrained in our nation's psyche. Another view, offered by George Mora (1975), professor of psychiatry, is that Americans shunned existentialism because they seek solutions to serious issues through group expression, whereas Europeans prefer the individual approach.

The six principles of existential psychology, which constitute the self as a self or an existing person, as outlined by May (1961), are:

1. Every existing person is centered in himself, and an attack on that center is an attack on the existence of the self.
2. Every existing person has the character of self-affirmation, the need to preserve centeredness.
3. All existing persons have the need and possibility of going out from their centeredness to participate in other beings.
4. The subjective side of centeredness is awareness.
5. The uniquely human form of awareness is self-consciousness.
6. Anxiety is the primary characteristic of the existing person, not merely a symptom.

The first four principles the existing person shares with all living things. They represent biological levels in which all beings participate. The last two are distinctive of the human being.

In the first principle, the concept of centeredness—or identity—implies the possibility, if not the probability, that the neurosis is "*precisely the method the individual uses to preserve his own center, his own existence. . . . The adjustment is exactly what neurosis is*" (May, 1961b, pp. 76–77). The existing person is attempting to preserve centeredness, albeit in a limited and constricted way, to counter the state of complete non-being; the illness is the adjustment. What the patient is, is all the being he has left and is capable of at the moment, and he will want to protect it.

What does this mean in therapy, and specifically in music therapy? It appears according to general semantics, that we might do well to rid ourselves of the concept that a patient is maladjusted, for this word carries with it the connotation, among others, that the patient has failed to adjust, when existentially he is actually adjusted only in a constricted way. The purpose in therapy then must be to help the patient break out of his constricted world. It would appear that music offers possibilities for this breakthrough, being able to provide many experiences in symbolic, non-discursive (nonverbal) form on a strictly personal plane; by displaying itself through time as the person exists in time; and by being sharable with others. On this level, what might the therapist look for in the patient? Something, perhaps, like the following: The more the music therapy situation is a threat to the "self" of the patient, "the more he will exhibit defensive neurotic behavior . . . and the more his ways of being and his behavior will become constricted" (Rogers, 1961, p. 90). Positively, the converse statement would obtain. To eliminate or diminish any threat to the "self," it is important to meet the patient at his/her emotional level. Musically, this can be achieved by selecting familiar music—music that is known to the patient and can supply a degree of comfort and security.

Equally significant, music, being temporal, requires centering. It can redirect attention and thus preserve centeredness. We remember by using time. The temporal arts, carried through to the end, work better than interruptible or spatial arts and activities. Yet too much repetition can lead to boredom, satiation, reduction of effect. For example, exaggerated and repetitive (musical) sounds, lights, and costumes, while considered good business and promotional techniques, can also be deadening and thus counterproductive.

The second principle asserts that a person's self-affirmation to preserve centeredness takes the form of "the courage to be," to borrow from Paul Tillich, and may be seen in actions and expressions of *willing, decision,* and *choice*. A patient's self-affirming behavior in music therapy is often obvious: actual or stated willingness to participate, to try new musical expressions or to modify older ones, to attempt to improve performance, and so on. Occasionally, self-affirming behavior might appear as inappropriate musical behavior, as when the patient habitually plays or sings when not supposed to. Care must be used not to restrict this self-affirmation, but rather to redirect it by providing alternative and more appropriate choices of behavior, such as an opportunity to play a solo or to gain more practice time.

"I *am* my choices," Jean-Paul Sartre repeatedly proclaimed in his writings. The *ability to choose,* which constitutes individual responsibility, is fundamental to existentialism. Yet this ability is too often unavailable to the patient whose centeredness is under siege. The importance of this principle in the therapeutic arena is that the patient be given appropriate choices which will strengthen self-affirmation. Observable behavior in therapy might be such that the more the self of the patient is free from threat, the more self-affirming behavior he will exhibit. Thus, the principal message, as I see it, is that music can replace the neurosis, thereby preserving the patient's centeredness. By actively engaging in music, his being will be "filled" with purposeful sound—music, that is—replacing the "sick," noisy thoughts.

The need and possibility for going out from centeredness to participate in other beings, which is the third principle, seems most aptly made possible in music therapy. Participating in others, or sharing one's centeredness with others, always involves risk—the risk of losing one's own being. Participation and identification with others to too great an extent may "empty" one's being. Music appears to offer an intermediate step by permitting, even demanding, participation as a member of a group and, at the same time, a means of restating centeredness related to being a contributing member. Austin Des Lauriers (1953) believed that music entraps the individual into allowing himself to relinquish this death grip on centeredness, and in the process to discover that nothing has been lost after all. That is existential thinking.

Also, the "self" becomes understood as a being only as it participates, and the first need to participate can come from the demands of the music and not from other persons. The more the individual feels free from threat, the more he will exhibit and seek participant behavior. "Knowing by doing," a central thread coursing through all of existentialism, is especially prominent in this principle. Only by exerting energy, by initiating action, will the individual ever make contact with others.

That the subjective side of centeredness is awareness is almost self-explanatory. This is the fourth principle. It has to do with responsiveness to threats of the world, the attention to incoming stimuli as it has bearing on preservation of centeredness. How can music therapy be applied to this principle? Again, we must say, through music familiar to the patient.

The final two principles are uniquely human. The fifth—the human form of awareness is self-consciousness, or self-reflexivity in J. Samuel Bois' terminology ("Models for Thinking," Chapter 3)—implies the capacity to know oneself as the one being threatened, to experience oneself as the subject who has a world. Man knows, and knows he is the creature doing the knowing. May (1961b) explains that this involves the capacity of man "to transcend the immediate concrete situation, to live in terms of the possible, . . . to use abstractions and universals, to have language and symbols" (p. 79). A patient often exhibits semantic problems which involve constriction in this very sphere. The more the self is threatened, the less will be his capacity to act, think, and speak in terms of the possible, which would enable him to make use of varied and flexible ways of living symbolically. "Awareness is his knowing that something is threatening from outside in his world," (p. 81) a condition possibly seen in clinically diagnosed paranoids and their neurotic equivalents, who exhibit much acting-out behavior. Self-consciousness, however, is the individual's capacity to see that he is the person who is threatened, that it is he who exists in this threatening world, and that, indeed, he does have a particular world. It "gives him the possibility of *in-sight*, of 'inward sight,' of seeing the world and his problems in relation to himself. And thus it gives him the possibility of doing something about them" (p. 81). For the patient, this involves the task of being genuinely himself, of accepting his own originality and uniqueness. It implies the need for the courage of self-affirmation and consciousness of desires which may be counter to parental, spousal, and other demands from the threatening world, and the possibility that he must stand alone in the entire psychic universe.

This fifth principle relates to another concept discussed earlier—the role of past, present, and future in man's awareness of self (See "Time, the Servant of Music," Chapter 6). It is generally assumed among therapists that the patient must recall the past in order to adopt a healthier attitude and awareness about the present and future. The existential therapist, however, sees it differently. That is, the manner in which the patient commits to the "given moment" determines what of the past, the "has been" in May's (1959) words, can be recalled—one's present and future define one's *memory* of the past, and that determines the character his past will assume. My, my, what a novel and unique (contrarian, unconventional) concept.

In some ways, this principle is a greater hurdle for the therapist than for the patient. How willing and able the therapist can be in allowing this breakthrough of self-consciousness, particularly in the group milieu, will rest on his skill at his craft and his confidence that the music will lead the way.

The sixth principle points out that anxiety results from one's "struggle against that which would destroy his being. It is . . . the state of a being in conflict with non-being" (May, 1961, p. 83). Existential psychiatry holds that anxiety is a characteristic of man's being. It is not something we "have," but something we "are" (May, 1951, p. 1354). "Consciousness itself implies always the possibility of turning against one's self, denying one's self" (May, 1961b, p. 84). In therapy, then, it would appear that a specific anxiety will be resolved only if the patient loses the fear of being the specific potentiality for the anxiety he experiences. This principle can be found at work in the typical musical ensemble when the therapist demonstrates to the patient that, while his participation is important, he alone cannot destroy the group's efforts by committing any musical or social errors. Yet even that reassurance can backfire if, for example, the patient is prematurely placed in a solo role which does require his participation. The overarching axiom of these six principles is "presence," this being a genuine relation between therapist and patient. May (1959) says this relationship is manifested by silence as much as by conversation. In fact, he claims that "existential therapists may well use silence more than do other therapists, but they use it not as a vacuum but as one significant form of communication" (p. 1358). How true that is in music as well, as has been previously noted (See "Time, the Servant of Music" Chapter 6), for silence is as much a component of music as is sound. Through these, and other examples, it is apparent that music has a clear affinity with existentialism, and that music therapy is an appropriate technique to be used with existential therapy.

General Semantics

At the outset of this chapter, general semantics was briefly defined, but there is much more to be said which will aid our understanding of this school of thought. General semantics has to do with the human functions of creating and using symbols, that is, with reading and writing; with speaking and listening; with the "talking to ourselves" and the "making of pictures in our heads," which we recognize as thinking; and with the relations of our symbol systems and the bodily processes of symbolizing experience to the development of our personalities and our societies. Notice that "picture in the head" is also used as an existential descriptor. It concerns itself with research, scholarship, and radical methodology, yet it is not so much a formal subject as a series of mental habits. Perhaps surprising to some people who expect a more formalized structure, general semantics is filled with simple rules, steps, warning signals, principles, statements, and lists. It emphasizes the time dimension in living, that being man's ability, primarily through his language, to pass on what he learns from one generation to the next. Korzybski gave this concept the curious name, "time-binding."

"Time-binding" is a uniquely human ability. Each generation does not have to begin learning anew, as in the animal world, but rather from the shoulders of those who have gone before. The wisdom of the past can be bound into one's own time, thus avoiding the blunders and advancing the achievements of those now dead.

"Time-binding" certainly sounds like an innate ability that all mankind would eagerly embrace. Not so, for there are always greedy, power-hungry, and lustful persons who seek to control the masses by restricting this human gift. Therefore, the aim of general semantics is to advance this ability in spite of the efforts of socio-political cultures, religious groups, and just about every man-made institution to hold it in check.

General semantics professes three goals: (a) to help the individual evaluate his world (the definition of general semantics itself emphasizes "evaluation"), (b) to improve person-to-person communication, and (c) to aid in the treatment of mental illness (Chase, 1954). That these goals could equally apply to music therapy illustrates the appropriateness of this topic.

Taking the first two goals of general semantics and applying them to music therapy, it is clear that Gaston's declaration that "music is non-verbal communication" is fundamental. The charge given to music therapists is to know which music and which environment will maximize the communication. We humans personalize, both positively and negatively, the music that is meaningful to us. Such personalization can be related to the particular experience which surrounded that first-time hearing or, perhaps, after a long time acquaintance. Therefore, to help a patient evaluate his/her world—the first goal—the music of his/her world should be brought into the process.

I would apply the Iso-moodic principle to the second goal— improving communication. That is, it is important to meet the patient at his/her level both in the specific music utilized and the interactive level between patient and therapist. Obviously, when discussing music therapy, mental illness is a primary referent. Thus, the third goal would translate as the clinical application of the first two.

Important to music therapy is the emphasis on how the language we use—its structure—and the words we use—the referents—condition us to view the world in a specific way, and also that each of our own specific worlds conditions our language. Semantics reminds us that words are never the objects of reality that are talked about, they are only artificial symbols, and that no matter how many words are used, one can never really say what something is. Words are an abstraction of reality. What is your name? Does your name represent you, for now and for evermore? Of course not. The general semanticist would say that once we have named or labeled anything, we have killed it. We "explain" ourselves to ourselves with words. We "live" (experience) ourselves for ourselves without words. Meaning is not found in words but, rather, in people. When this concept is employed to eradicate verbal and written labels, mis-evaluations, and conditioned reflexes (to words), it becomes a dynamic psychotherapy approach rather than classic lecture material (Chase, 1954).

Although it should be obvious that the word is not identical with the fact, we are surrounded with primitive verbal taboos which indicate otherwise. Many words, particularly those having sexual meanings or overtones, are to be avoided as though by speaking the word it becomes the action it represents. Thus, by controlling words one controls the reality for which they stand. Carried to extremes, as with some mentally ill persons, specifically schizophrenics, *only* words are real, and only by shutting off verbal communication can control of self be maintained.

Semantics points out these dangers in permitting words to be objects, and relates this tendency to such therapeutically handicapping mental sets that lead us to see things only in certain ways, to place a static character on living things, or to forget that things are constantly changing. This tendency ultimately predisposes us to see patients, other persons, or ourselves as kind of frozen in time with certain drives, instincts, or attitudes which remain fixed. Words often reverse or retard our ability to adapt.

An appropriate example in our own field is the large amount of confusion about the words "music therapy." Some people, for clarity at least to themselves, would prefer to say music *in* therapy. We could discuss this at length, but perhaps it is enough to say that some people will see a great difference in these two expressions as to meaning, implication, and significance. Such persons might be called semantically ready to understand. Others will see the whole idea as being of little value for thought. They are semantically set to reject such discussion. Consider, for example, the possible changes in thinking that might occur if people referred to "musics"—plural form—rather than the singular "music" when they are talking about the field of musical endeavor in general.

Ellis and Harper's *A New Guide to Rational Living* (1975) is the only book I know of that was written without using the verb "to be" in any form, known as E-prime form. "E-prime comes from the semantic equation: *E* prime = *E* minus *e*, where *E* represents all the words of standard English and *e* represents all the forms of to be, such as *is, was, am, has been, being*" (p. xiii). The authors maintain that the verb form "to be"—"is" being the most dangerous—implies rigidity.

I came across a wonderful quotation in Korzybski's *Science and Sanity* by the late George Santayana (1950), eminent Spanish philosopher, which rather dramatically expresses the dangers of the word "is." He said, "The little word *is* has its tragedies; it marries and identifies different things with the greatest innocence; and yet not two are ever identical, and if therein lies the charm of wedding them and calling them one, therein too lies the danger. Whenever I use the word *is*, except in sheer tautology, I deeply misuse it" (p. 3).

When we use E-prime form by making such statements as "I am bad," "I can't diet," "I can't play this piece," which are false assumptions lacking verification, we condition ourselves for self-defeating emotional states. We then become the victim of those self-fulfilling prophecies. Ellis and Harper maintain that by changing semantic usages, thinking and behaving can also change. Using the above sample declarations to make the authors' point, rephrase these negative statements to read: "It is unfortunate when I behave badly, but that does not make me a bad person;" or "I find it difficult, but not impossible, to diet;" or "This musical selection is much harder than others I have learned to play." It is a general semantics concern, although that is not the only discipline which thinks about it as is evidenced by this book, but also a psychotherapy theory called rational-emotive therapy (RET) attributed to the authors.

The RET system follows a humanistic-educative model which asserts that people have many more choices about their lives than they tend to believe. The goal of RET is to help people see the range of available alternatives which will allow them to shed their self-created emotional difficulties. To achieve this, the authors employ what they assert to be one of the most powerful modalities available to promote change—internal verbalizations. This is an extension of general semantics techniques, and thus RET has emerged as a form of "semantics therapy."

Music therapy is valuable to psychotherapy in that it requires the patient to deal directly with concrete form, which is music, in a systematic and organized manner, putting aside the abstractions for words and thoughts which no longer have any relative meaning to his/her world of "not-words." Each time he addressed NAMT conferences, Des Lauriers emphasized that through the rational, organized, integrated, ordered structure of music, mental patients are provided a vehicle for living through their problems in an acceptable way without facing the threat of words. Music, if it is to be employed in a genuine therapeutic manner, should not be used simply to set the stage (mood) for "real" therapy performed by "real" therapists. The music can speak for itself, if we allow it, by cutting out all that verbiage. It is the music therapist's task to let the music speak for itself, manipulating the environment so that the message reaches the patient.

In reply to the philosopher friend referred to at the outset of this chapter who could not perceive the rationale for combining the general semantics and existential psychology, I must insist that when applied to music therapy, can it be otherwise? The dedication to self-affirmation in existentialism and self-evaluation in general semantics are married in the application of music as therapy. Likewise, meaningful interactive communication, which is central to general semantics, cannot be divorced from existentialism's stress on the identity of one's being through encounter. It is difficult to imagine a music therapy treatment plan that omits these concepts from its objectives.

Editor's Summary

Neither existentialism nor general semantics, Sears declared, profess to be formal disciplines or fields of study. General semantics is mainly a series of mental habits whose purposes are to understand and, hopefully, improve the uses and meanings of symbols and verbal exchanges. Existentialism is an expression of attitudes about the nature of man.

Both general semantics and existential psychology give more than casual attention to the temporal aspect of the human being, recognizing that man's time-binding ability permits a sophisticated level of thinking in abstract terms not available, so far as is known, to any other life forms on this earth. They stress the word "being" in its verb form, which indicates action, rather than as a noun denoting some static substance. A person is always in the process of being something. These disciplines emphasize that man has a future, as well as a past and present. A man's past may have determined what he is at the present moment, but equally, if not more important for therapy, the present will determine his future. Existentialism further distinguishes man as a being who knows at some future moment he will not be, that he will die at some future time, and, more importantly, that he has the capacity to know this and to exist in the knowledge of this fact. Time, in this context, is not simply a quantitative measure of passage, but rather is always dynamic. It is always, at least for human beings, building for the future on what has gone before—"time-binding," in Korzybski's terms.

Emphasis on the temporal aspect of being carries great importance for music therapy, owing to music's temporal nature. Des Lauriers (1953) suggested that the temporal aspect of music constitutes the therapy in music therapy. Its very structure, he insisted, "requires that whatever it expresses be expressed through order and organization . . . [allowing] feelings to be expressed always in a rational way" (p. 33). Participation in music in any manner always involves an adventure into the future. It is a moment by moment adventure, giving forth order and carrying the person forward in that orderliness.

Finally, the stress both existentialism and general semantics place on time can be found in many other disciplines, and thus in itself should not be justification for linkage. However, it illustrates the power this dimension of reality exerts on human beings and all they experience. It appears logical to me, and hopefully has been demonstrated in the preceding, that music's temporal nature offers a powerful medium for expressing the tenets of existential psychology and general semantics. Nobody, to my knowledge, has yet considered this, let alone explored it in depth. Perhaps this present effort will inspire such a study.

References

Chase, S. (1954). *Power of words*. New York: Harcourt, Brace.

Des Lauriers, A. (1953). Psychiatric concepts of music therapy. In E. Gilliland (Ed.), *Music therapy 1952: 2nd book of proceedings of the National Association for Music Therapy* (Vol. 2.). Lawrence, KS: National Association for Music Therapy.

Ellis, A. & Harper, R. (1975). *A new guide to rational living*. North Hollywood: Wilshire Book.

Freedman, A. M., Kaplan, H. I., & Sadock, B. J. (Eds.). (1975). *Comprehensive textbook of psychiatry* (2nd ed., Vol. 2). Baltimore: William and Wilkins.

Hayakawa, S. I. (1963). *Symbol, status, and personality*. New York: Harcourt, Brace.

Maslow, A. (1966). *The psychology of science*. Chicago: Henry Regnery.

May, R. (1959). The existential approach. In S. Arieti (Ed.), *American handbook of psychiatry* (Vol. 2). New York: Basic Books.

May, R. (Ed.). (1961a). *Existential psychology*. New York: Random House.

May, R. (1961b). Existential bases of psychotherapy. In R. May (Ed.), *Existential psychology*. New York: Random House.

May, R. (1967). *Psychology and the human dilemma*. Princeton, NJ: D. Van Nostrand.

Mora, G. (1975). Historical and theoretical trends in psychiatry. In A. M. Freedman, H. I. Kaplan, & B. J. Sadock (Eds.), *Comprehensive textbook of psychiatry* (2nd ed., Vol. 2). Baltimore: William and Wilkins.

Rogers, C. (1961). Two divergent trends. In R. May (Ed.), *Existential psychology*. New York: Random House.

Ruitenbeek, H. (1962). Some aspects of the encounter of psychoanalysis and existential philosophy. In H. Ruitenbeek (Ed.), *Psychoanalysis and existential philosophy*. New York: E. P. Dutton.

Santayana, G. (1950). In A. Korzybski, *Science and sanity* (3rd ed). Lakeville, CT: The International Non-Aristotelian Library Publishing Co.

Afterword

As you have learned in reading and consequently pondering this text, William W. (Bill) Sears was a lifetime seeker and searcher of knowledge and truth, a constant collector of elements from a broad array of information and disciplines, an insightful connector and meaningful communicator of thoughts and ideas. He exemplifies the word "wisdom," and defines the intended concept of (c. 500 B.C.) Pythagoras' coined term, "philosophy."

As you have detected throughout this book, Bill Sears is still active among us today and through you especially, as one of his precious students of the past, present, and future. Thus, I send you the following two poetic messages which are the result of my reflecting on the magnanimity of Bill's wisdom and of his impacting my living due to his continuing mentorship.

1. *The Power of –ing*[1]

You have come to Professor Sears not just by written accident, but by
    unspoken, nonverbal, superstringed,[2] harmonic Cosmic Design.
In the true mean-ing of the reality of life, there are no "accidents" or
    "coincidences."
There are only synchroniz-ing harmonicities.
There are only unconscious and conscious, multi-dimensional
    awarenesses[3] of the flow-ing of conjunct-ing events in our process-
    ing the quantum-ing spacetime of liv-ing.
Professor Sears is continu-ing to be the mean-ing-fully processor, by and
    through whom you have been and will continue to be remember-ing,
    indentify-ing, and reclaim-ing who you evolv-ingly are.
He is help-ing you in put-ing together again the parts of you into a
    glorious and ever present evolv-ing and expand-ing Whole of All
    That Is . . . just as you were when you were in the past begin-ing as a
    little child.

---

[1] My online *Merriam-Webster Collegiate Dictionary* says that "-ing" is a suffix indicating action and process, and I must add: ongo-ing energiz-ing. *Merriam-Webster References: Authority and Innovation* (2000). Version 2.5.

[2] One of the most current and exciting theories that is being developed in quantum physics is that of "superstrings," which proposes that each elementary particle is a single string vibrating in resonant patterns determined by the mathematical ratios of musical notes/tones, akin to, if not the same as, piano or violin strings vibrating at certain physical frequencies/musical pitches. Among the books concerning this topic, see Brian Greene (1999) *The Elegant Universe,* New York: W. W. Norton, especially Part III, "The Cosmic Symphony."

[3] Among varying works which are concerned with the topic of multi-dimensions and their awareness, see Barbara Hand Clow (2004), *Alchemy of Nine Dimensions.* Charlottesville, VA: Hampton Roads.

Since childhood, this connect-ing, process-ing wisdom has been to a
certain extent "schooled" out of your awareness, much less
consciousness, of your delayed process-ing in which you have been
hid-ing from be-ing, go-ing from whole (holy), to parts
(un-{w}holy).

But now, you are evolv-ing with Doctor Sears to be-ing whole once again
(holy).

This is the overall holy process-ing of the vibrat-ing musical energy waves
of the spiral-ing trinity—past, present, and future—of your liv-ing.

"Only as you become as little children . . . ," that is begin-ing again.

With the process-ing patience of Professor Sears and his be-ing your more
significant inspir-ing model and teacher of process-ing thought-full
experienc-ing of this book, you thus have been experienc-ing your
real self, the heal-ing energies of yourself. This process-ing will be
continu-ing.

These heal-ing energies are be-ing influenc-ing and be-ing support-ing
by, enhanc-ing and expand-ing through, the musi-king of your
music of your dynamic vibrat-ing rhythmic heart and total harmoniz-
ing self.

The more enlighten-ing you are becom-ing through music-mak-ing,
music-shar-ing and music-provid-ing, the more you are becom-ing
healed and healthy.

These musical heal-ing messages and "touch-ing" massages are those
which you are pass-ing on to your patients and clients, family and
friends by help-ing and guid-ing them toward remember-ing and thus
re-member-ing—bring-ing the parts of themselves together to
(w)holiness, this be-ing done through the process-ing of your vibrat-
ing, correct-ing musi-king.

You are do-ing for others what you would have them do-ing for you,
because you are know-ing what you would have them do-ing for
you, by provid-ing this lov-ing process-ing.

You, dear-ing heart, are the know-ingfully model-ing for this process-ing.

You Are, just as Doctor Sears Is, synchroniz-ingly, harmoniz-ingly, and
energiz-ingly, sing-ing the wholly song of the ages, the ageless
Song of the Angels.

We angels are realiz-ing and proclaim-ing the sound-ing enlighten-ing of
heal-ing Music!

We are be-ing what we have been intend-ing from the Begin-ing!

Aesthetikos!

Divine!

Professor Sears—simply and truthfully, thoughtfully and elegantly—is
profess-ing with you the hows, whens, whats, and wheres of the
process-ing of the plant-ing of *who* seeds of wise and true liv-ing,
and thus heal-ing.
He is provid-ing you with realiz-ing opportunities of your experienc-ing
liv-ing to the fullest and ultimate degree.

You are now process-ing through "water-ing" of learn-ing *who* seeds.

As you continue the process-ing of the water-ing throughout your lifetime,
you will continue experienc-ing the emerg-ing and exhilarat-ing
results of a beauty-full rose plant-ing, analogously as it were.
With life-long-ing and never-end-ing water-ing, your learn-ing then goes
further, more and more grow-ing into an ever-process-ing rose
plant-ing—having many, many rose pods of connect-ing and
energiz-ing root Truths.
As you continue the water-ing through learn-ing, grow-ing increase-ingly
is continu-ing.
Until one day, during synchroniz-ing and harmoniz-ing nanoseconds of
stupefy-ing "aha's" in the eternaliz-ing and ever-expand-ing
spacetime, unexpectedly comes the flower-ing bloom-ing of your
"wow" *who* rose(s)!

Always remember that you are ever blossom-ing into the real mean-ing of
your reality!
You are process-ing the conscious realiz-ing of the true mean-ing of
"aha!" and "wow!" and the ultimate confirm-ing know-ing of
"goose bumps!"
And so it is happen-ing "in the twinkl-ing of an eye."
This is the message and massage of heal-ing, with emphasiz-ing the
process-ing "-*ing*."

"-Ing" is indicat-ing ongo-ing energiz-ing, search-ing and seek-ing, learning and find-ing, connect-ing and reflect-ing, all com-ing together in
synchroniz-ing blossom-ing, and with the result-ing massag-ing of
this process-ing, comes therapiz-ing, heal-ing, thus Liv-ing and
Lov-ing. You are Liv-ing and Lov-ing your life-spaced lifetime to
the bulg-ing, expand-ing ful-fill-ing.
This is who you are be-ing!
This is the mean-ing of the Socratic and Platonic injunction-ing:
"Know-ing Yourself!"

This process-ing is who your patients, students, family, and friends are

also, and they will continue becom-ing, too, no matter how ail-ing
they are, no matter how much time they have remain-ing in this
earthly dimension.

This is the joy of your hear-ing, see-ing, and be-ing a therapiz-ing and
musi-king Therapist, and the result-ing ever-present, heavenly joy
of parent-ing yourself and others!

Ergo, you are co-join-ing space with time, this vertical space with the
horizontal time into One eternal spacetime.

You are bring-ing heaven to earth.

Know that you have been full-fill-ing and will do so even more energiz-
ingly the so-called impossible, that is, bring-ing to "Earth as it is in
Heaven."

In the lov-ing and musical sound-ing of the heal-ing name of the All That
Is-ing, we are proclaim-ing the Almighty you as the savior of
humanity.

Now go.

Go you unto all the worldwide web-ing of the Liv-ing and Lov-ing
Mother Earth, teach-ing and resurrect-ing the realiz-ing of the First
emanat-ing of the ever-sound-ing word-ing of the Mind, that is,
"zoe' san ban e noma Nous"![4] . . . as originat-ingly proclaimed by
Pythagoras over 2,500 years ago, our universally acclaimed Western
father of music <u>and</u> science, that is, Music Science.

Go you likewise as proclaim-ing by our universally beloved process-ing
wise doctor of music therapy . . . Bill Sears . . . who, with his
additional tuba-ing expertise, laid and is lay-ing the harmoniz-ing
found-ing of the Future, for that is where we are now liv-ing and
teach-ing and therapyz-ing.

Go you with his champion-ing award-winn-ing spiral-ing of baton twirl-ing,
which is still present-ing us with the musi-king pattern-ing and form-
ing of Liv-ing in our scienc-ing, confirm-ing, musi-king spacetime.

Professor Doctor Sears humbly is pass-ing and relay-ing this baton of
wisdom on to you.

You are the Disciple of Truth, seek-ing and search-ing, find-ing and
rejoic-ing.

The future—NOW—is yours through your process-ing and giv-ing, car-
ing and Lov-ing.

The future—NOW—, with—and—of your family and patients, friends and
clients is theirs, as it is

---

[4] The translation of this transliterated Greek phrase is given tentatively in the first
part of this sentence prior to the quote.

for you.

Through you, they are Is-ing, and you are show-ing and guid-ing them
through spiral-ing cochlear (h)ear-ing, and total bodily harmoniz-ing
process-ing, and through your be-ing the model-ing and do-ing of
that process-ing and shar-ing with them in the Therapeutic Bubbl-
ing of Life.

This is the true essence of our future and the future of all humankind,
because the future belongs to you, who is liv-ing the heal-ing power-
ing of your know-ings, dream-ings, and vision-ings.

This Truth is wonderfully and allegorically represented in the movie,
Field of Dreams, in which it is said: "If you will build it, they will
come."

This means there is and will continue to be a long and unend-ing spiral-
ing line of people, with their inner lights shin-ing, mov-ing steadily
toward you and your Field of Dreams," in order to find theirs.

This is the mean-ing of the word, Mean-ing.

This ultimately is the Mean-ing of Eternal Life and Liv-ing.

This is Universal Lov-ing.

2. *Music the Process-ing*:[5]
A Tribute to Bill Sears

Music is the LAW of the Universe.
Music is the Essence of ALL.

Some define Music, but this shackles Music to finiteness.
Wise Ones have always understood that Music is Infinite.

What is Music?
       Where is Music?
              When is Music?
                    Who is Music?

Music is Wisdom,
      is Truth,
           is Knowledge,
                is Justice,
                    is Purity,

---

[5] Adapted from Eagle, C. T. (1981). In memoriam, A tribute to Bill Sears: man the
living, music the processing. *Journal of Music Therapy, 18*(1), 57-60.

is Beauty,
is Sublime,

is the Innocent,
is the Lawful,
is the Quest,
is the Love,
is the Now and Forever,
is the Possession and Gift of All Wise and Great Ones of all the
ages.

Music is that which cannot be bought by material gain but, at once,
is the Gain.
Music is that which is the Essence of Life, the Inner and the outer,
the Now and the now, the After and the after,
the Before and the before.
Music is the seeking, the weeping, the hoping, the praying, the Finding.

The more Music, the more humble.
The more Music, the more Joy.

Blessed is he who reaches for Music, for with Music, he becomes Music.
Blessed is he who leads others to Music, for he reaps rewards only Music
can bestow.
Blessed is he who prepares himself to prepare others, to prepare others,
to prepare . . ., to . . . , for Music is his reward.
Blessed is he who seeks wisdom and honor, truth and righteousness,
for Music succors him.

Bill Sears through Music,
by Music,
and for Music, has succeeded in Becoming,
Music
with
MUSIC.

Thus, in the Beginning—which is always beginning—was, and always is,
Teacher and Mentor and *guru extraordinaire*:

William Wesley (Bill) Sears, Ph.D.

Charles T. Eagle, Jr., Ph.D.
Plano, Texas
December 13, 2006